Hemingway in Comics

Hemingway in Comics

Robert K. Elder

with Sharon Hamilton, Jace Gatzemeyer, and Sean C. Hadley

The Kent State University Press

Kent, Ohio

For Dylan and Eva,

who grew up in

Hemingway's hometown,

surrounded by comic books

© 2020 by The Kent State University Press, Kent, Ohio 44242
All rights reserved
ISBN 978-1-60635-400-1
Manufactured in Canada

Cataloging information for this title is available at the Library of Congress.

24 23 22 21 20   5 4 3 2 1

Contents

Foreword

Brian Azzarello

Whenever I'm asked about my biggest influences, I always say Raymond Chandler, William Faulkner, and Ernest Hemingway. Now, if you know my work, that last bearded guy might not be an obvious choice. There are no homages or references to him in my comics.

But Hemingway shaped me as a writer, and as a writer of comics specifically.

Let me start at the beginning. My first experience with Hemingway was when I was six. My uncle Elmer made me watch *The Old Man and the Sea* movie with him. I didn't like it as much as he did. For a six-year-old, it's kind of a boring movie, except the shark part. The whole theme of the movie was lost on me immediately. I asked Uncle Elmer, "Why didn't the old man just let that fish go?"

He tucked me into bed, said, "Bahhhh," and waved a hand at me.

But now I understand why the old man didn't let the fish go—because the fish isn't a fish!

The Old Man and the Sea is very simple and tribal. Great literature tends to be simple—elementally simple—and lends itself to graphic storytelling. Comics operate on a similar level. Why does Batman work as an iconic character? Because he is defined in elemental terms. He hangs around at night. He wears black.

Elementally, Hemingway writes and drinks and wears that sweater. It's the image Sloppy Joe's Bar in Key West uses. For better or worse, that's what the shorthand has become, the iconography. Unfortunately, his myth tends to overshadow his writing, so people form an opinion of Hemingway without reading his work. I knew who he was before I knew what he did. But once I learned what he did, I started to appreciate him. His stories are fantastic; they still have a pulse.

Like everyone else, I read him in high school. First, *The Sun Also Rises*, and then I started reading his other work on my own. What I like about *The Sun Also Rises* is that Hemingway isn't telling you exactly what is happening—the aimlessness, the promiscuity, Jake's mysterious injury, etc. The moral structure of the time had something to do with that. Hemingway couldn't come out and say exactly what was going on. But I understood it—or I thought I did. With Hemingway, you become a really active reader.

Comics make a similar demand on you. You, the reader, are part of the language of comics. You have to fill in a lot of blanks, and the space between panels. These are static images that really move when you're inside the story and things start to pick up speed.

Through Hemingway, I learned to celebrate weakness in my characters. Almost every character in *The Sun Also Rises* is weak in some regard. That's what the Lost Generation is about: Life is a party when life has no meaning. I'd argue that all the Minutemen in my series *100 Bullets* share this profile. They're killers who behave on the surface—by nature of their jobs—like life has no meaning. Only rather than being broken by a war, they've been fractured by personal tragedies.

Hemingway's characters have rich inner lives, so their actions have meaning. When I've talked to younger writers about characters with inner lives, sometimes they look at me like I'm speaking a foreign language. Well-written characters never act out of character because they have such a strong inner light. Even if you're not getting into their heads, their words and actions tell you who they are.

Take gunrunner Harry Morgan in Hemingway's *To Have and Have Not*. On the surface, he's brutal and compromised, but in reality, he's a moral, strong character. He's doing wrong things for right reasons. My own Agent Graves in *100 Bullets* certainly fits that definition.

Comic book writers can learn a lot from Hemingway. There's only so much room you have in a panel for dialog, and, in dialog, there's nobody better than Hemingway for saying the most with the least amount of words. I wish more of my colleagues knew that. Some of these guys act like they're getting paid by the word.

Hemingway's characters rarely exactly say what they mean, which means you have to interpret what they say. For instance, with *The Sun Also Rises,* you could ask three different people what the ending means, and you'd get three different answers. The storytelling makes you a participant.

So, go out there and participate. Read Hemingway's original work and see what sparked the people in this book to make him a part of their comics.

And remember, the fish isn't a fish.

Introduction

Robert K. Elder

From Thierry Murat's adaptation of *Le Vieil Homme et La Mer* (*The Old Man and the Sea*) (2014). Used with permission of the artist.

Comic book creators and Hemingway share a natural kinship. The comic book page demands an economy of words, and—for multi-panel stories—a lot of the action takes place between the panels. It's an interactive reading experience, much like Hemingway's work. It demands that you interpret and bring yourself to the text, like Hemingway's less-is-more "iceberg theory," in graphic form.

In *Death in the Afternoon* (1932), Hemingway expounded on his theory that what is left out of a story gives it power, that the act of omission strengthens a story. Hemingway contends that in the hands of a talented writer, a reader "will have a feeling of those things as strongly as though the writer had stated them. The dignity of movement of an ice-berg is due to only one-eighth of it being above water." Comic book artists and writers similarly make choices that require both surface and thematic readings, with narrative information being absorbed through a spare, meticulous pairing of text and artwork. Done well, comics are visual experiences that plumb emotional depths.

Hemingway's influence continues to permeate pop culture, and comics are no exception.

While researching my book *Hidden Hemingway: Inside the Ernest Hemingway Archives of Oak Park,* I started collecting Hemingway references in pop culture, including more than 40 appearances in comic books. That research turned into several articles for the *Comics Journal* and the online *Hemingway Review.* To date, I've cataloged more than 120 Hemingway appearances, references, jokes, adaptations, homages, and doppelgängers from across the globe—and the list keeps growing. Even as I write this introduction, a colleague has just sent me a new story starring Hemingway from a comic book artist in Croatia.

Celebrity appearances aren't new to comic books. Both Stephen Colbert and President Barack Obama got guest shots with Spider-Man, and Eminem got a two-issue series with the Punisher. Orson Welles helped Superman foil a Martian invasion, and President John F. Kennedy helped the Man of Steel keep his secret identity. Even David Letterman got a studio visit from the Avengers. But, using the crowd-sourced Comic Book Database (comicbookdb.com) and my own research, I've discovered that Hemingway by far exceeds other authors in number of appearances (Shakespeare: 22, Mark Twain: 13). As historical figures go, only Abraham Lincoln comes close to touching him, with roughly 122 appearances in comics (and counting).

Hemingway casts a long shadow in literature, one that extends into comic books. In my first wave of research, I found him battling Fascists alongside Wolverine, playing poker with Harlan Ellison, and leading a revolution in Purgatory in *The Life After.* He has also appeared alongside Mickey Mouse, Captain Marvel, Cerebus, Lobo—even a Jazz Age Creeper. In comics, the Nobel Prize winner is often treated with equal parts reverence, curiosity, and parody.

In 2011, on the fiftieth anniversary of Hemingway's death, Reed Johnson wrote about how the author's image had been treated in pop culture. Writing for the *Los Angeles Times,* Johnson reflected on the "Hemingway caricature handed down to posterity: a hard-drinking, womanizing, big-game trophy-hunting, fame-craving blowhard who pushed his obsession about writing in a lean, mean prose style to the point of self-parody."

Five decades after Hemingway's death, Johnson observes, "There's another, more serious and respectable Hemingway still duking it out with this comic imposter in the ring of public perception."

That fight continues and is unlikely to be won anytime soon, because as author Tim O'Brien has pointed out, there is more than one Ernest Hemingway. In the many appearances I found, Hemingway is often the hypermasculine legend of Papa: bearded, boozed up, and ready to throw a punch. Just as often, comic book creators see past the bravado, to the sensitive artist looking for validation. This book endeavors to explore these Hemingway appearances, from the divine to the ridiculous.

When I first presented my research at the 2016 International Hemingway Conference in Oak Park, Illinois, I joked that this project was a pop culture rabbit hole that I couldn't climb out of. The statement grew truer as I was invited to give talks at universities and to host gallery showings. What I found was a curiosity among fans and scholars about Hemingway and how his legend gets recorded, distorted, parodied, and boiled down to its essential parts.

Hemingway has turned out to be the perfect avatar for comic book artists wanting to tell history-rich stories. He passed through the most beautiful places during the most chaotic times: Paris in the 1920s, Spain during the Spanish Civil War, Cuba on the brink of revolution, France in World War I and in World War II just after the Allies landed in Normandy. He is a fixed point and iconic touchstone that comic book creators love to invent stories around. Even when he's not the center of the book, a cameo appearance injects the story with energy and pathos.

Although Hemingway was an avid reader of newspapers, he seemed not to linger in the comics section—or, at least, he never wrote about it. His former secretary (and later daughter-in-law) Valerie Hemingway said that while he consumed multiple newspapers, he seemed to skip the comics.

He certainly knew that he was caricatured in his high school yearbook and mentioned in a few single-panel *New Yorker* cartoons before his death. He was also a consummate doodler; his mother kept some of his cartoonish sketches for his family scrapbooks. He was fond of drawing wine glasses and beer steins in letters, and notably, the teenage Hemingway drew a caricature of himself in a letter to family in 1918 after being wounded in World

Hemingway and his typewriter. By Gavin Aung Than, www.zenpencils.com.

Hemingway knocks out Jack Kerouac in this piece by Steve Rolston, commissioned by Joshua Wiebe for his brother Sam Wiebe. "It was my brother's birthday, and at the time we both hated Kerouac and found his writing style tedious, and loved Hemingway," Joshua Wiebe remembers. "He still has this drawing on his wall."

Artist Rolston says: "Personally, I have no ill will towards Kerouac. But I'd definitely put my money on Hemingway." Courtesy Steve Rolston. Reprinted with permission.

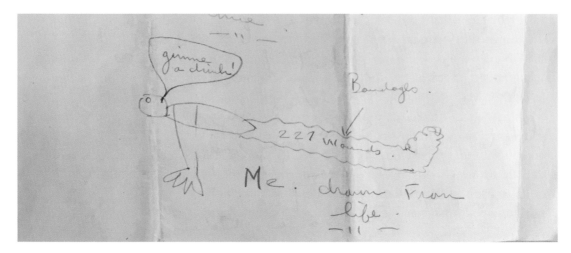

Hemingway's comic self-portrait while convalescing in Italy, in a letter dated July 21, 1918, now in the collection of the Lilly Library at Indiana University. Photo by Robert K. Elder.

Facing page: A fitting page about bullfighting from *Blondie and Dagwood Family* #4 (New York: Harvey Comics, 1963), 12. From the private collection of Robert K. Elder.

War I while working for the American Red Cross in Italy. He even includes a word balloon, "gimme a drink," and points to the 227 pieces of shrapnel taken out of his legs.

The only comic strip to which he was compared in his lifetime, however, was *Blondie*. After a 1952 visit to Hemingway's home in Cuba, Howard Berk wrote in *National Geographic* that Hemingway and his fourth wife, Mary, "seemed to be measuring each other. I had the distinct feeling that she was displeased and that he was trying to figure out what he had done. For some odd reason, the image that came to mind was Blondie and Dagwood, although neither resembled either."

This was a standard trope in the *Blondie* newspaper strip: the clueless husband trying to figure out why his wife was mad at him. For the unfamiliar, Chic Young's *Blondie* follows the courtship—and later marital conflicts of—bookkeeper Dagwood Bumstead and former flapper Blondie. Young's iconic couple translated their loving but friction-filled marriage from newspapers into radio, TV, movies, and their own monthly comic books published by Harvey Comics.

There's plenty of Hemingway the adventurer in the comics discussed in the following pages; there's also Hemingway the husband, the lover, the writer, the hunter, and a man alone, battling his demons.

A note about organization: I've largely kept to a chronological presentation, so it's easy to track Hemingway's evolution in comics. I have not differentiated between daily comic strips, like *Peanuts* and *Doonesbury,* single-panel *New Yorker*–style cartoons, and traditional comic books, like *Superman.* I've included comics and illustrations from big publishers (such as Marvel and DC), independents (such as Dark Horse Comics and Fantagraphics), and foreign publishers (Le Lombard, Manga Bungo, Panini), as well as underground, internet, and other self-published comics.

In an effort to be more inclusive and expand the scholarship, I've also included web comics and the odd subgenre of Hemingway as a portfolio

From Thierry Murat's adaptation of *Le Vieil Homme et La Mer* (*The Old Man and the Sea*) (2014). Used with permission of the artist.

model. While I was searching for images, I kept running into portraits of Hemingway and scenes from his work that weren't attached to either a book or a web comic. Rather, these commercial or portfolio images were created by aspiring comic book and graphic artists.

This work also includes a few breakout chapters, in which my collaborators offer examinations of Hemingway comics and adaptations. In a couple places I've grouped similar sections together, such as Italian Disney comics and the work of Norwegian cartoonist Jason.

Almost all of the interviews in this volume are original, appearing for the first time. In some places, I've removed my own questions and let the creators speak for themselves.

It's worth noting that this is not a complete encyclopedia of Hemingway in comics. That would be an impossible task, as a new work is always being created or found. To paraphrase Paul Simon, Hemingway has not ended up a cartoon in a cartoon graveyard. I see this not as the definitive work on the subject, but the first step.

Chicagoland, 2020

A Note about That Sweater

For Superman, it's the giant *S* on his chest. For John Lennon, it's a New York City T-shirt. For Ernest Hemingway, it's a bulky turtleneck sweater. So many comic book artists have adapted this image that it deserves an exploration of why it's so iconic.

Famed photographer Yousuf Karsh traveled to Cuba in March 1957 for a two-day shoot with Hemingway. He described the meeting in his 1960 book, *Portraits of Greatness:* "I expected to meet in the author a composite of the heroes of his novels," Karsh later recalled. "Instead . . . I found a man of peculiar gentleness, the shyest man I ever photographed—a man cruelly battered by life, but seemingly invincible."

Hemingway in March 1957. © Yousuf Karsh. Used with permission of the Karsh estate. All rights reserved. Karsh.org.

Karsh told *Chicagoland Magazine* in 1967 that Hemingway was "a very sad man, very melancholy, but he had a wonderful face—and that magnificent beard."

Karsh couldn't have known that he was capturing the author's likeness just four years before his death. The portrait was taken during one of the worst years of Hemingway's life. He was still recovering from the effects of back-to-back plane crashes in Africa in 1954. He was battling depression, high cholesterol, and high blood pressure. To add insult to his many injuries, Hemingway's doctors insisted that he stop drinking. It was "a dismal time for Ernest," wrote his friend and editor A. E. Hotchner in *Papa Hemingway,* his memoir of their relationship.

The mix of pensive sadness and Hemingway's weather-beaten face took on an aura that was "downright biblical," wrote Frederick Voss in his book *Picturing Hemingway.*

The 1989 US stamp of Hemingway, designed by M. Gregory Rudd. © United States Postal Service. All rights reserved.

Dr. Andrew Farah, in his 2017 book *Hemingway's Brain,* saw something else: "the clues to [Hemingway's] demise are evident: the famous scar on his left forehead is still visible, there is a heaviness above his eyelids, and his eyes peer out at slightly different angles, indicating a degree of neurological damage."

The cable-knit sweater that makes him look like an Irish longshoreman isn't a working-class statement—it's an expensive designer sweater from Christian Dior. Depending on who is telling the story, the sweater was either personally made for him by Dior or a Christmas gift his wife Mary bought in Dior's Paris boutique. Also, depending on the storyteller, the sweater's color was either green or brown suede.

Originally meant for *Life* magazine, the photo was later published in the *Atlantic Monthly* and a variety of magazines. It would become Hemingway's most recognized portrait and the basis for a stamp issued in 1989 by the United States Postal Service. Stamp designer M. Gregory Rudd used the central elements of Karsh's photo and set Hemingway against a backdrop of African plains.

While so many pop figures are immortalized in their youth (Elvis Presley, Jack Kerouac), Hemingway's end-of-life portrait became the most famous author photograph of all time. In comics, it's the most reproduced and symbolic representation of the man. Over the years, the sweater has become less a sweater and more a uniform, an iconic suit of armor—a costume.

Captain America has his cowl and star-spangled shield. Hemingway has that sweater.

Jef Mallet's *Frazz* comic strip from Monday, February 11, 2019. *Frazz* © 2019 Jef Mallett. Dist. By ANDREWS MCMEEL SYNDICATION. Reprinted with permission. All rights reserved.

1917–1960

Hemingway's High School Yearbook to *Tintin*

Senior Tabula (1917)

Hemingway's depiction as a comic character came early, in his senior-year high school yearbook, the *Senior Tabula,* published by Oak Park and River Forest High School in 1917. In fact, Hemingway shows up here as a cartoon character three times.

On page 138, in a comic titled *Some Things We'll Miss,* Hemingway appears next to the words "Ernie's Divine Form?!!" In the drawing, by sophomore Mae F. Parker, Hemingway stands awkwardly—with stubbly legs and hair tucked under a swimming cap—atop a diving board. On the sidelines, his classmates rib him, "Atta boy cupid!"

Another comic, titled *Our Ideas of Heaven,* features a newspaper sports page that reads "Hemingway Stars / Wins Plunge / and / Breaks End of Tank." In parentheses under the illustration, a caption reads, "Ah!—this is true fame."

Detail of Hemingway in a comic during school. *Senior Tabula,* 1917.

Hemingway's own idea of heaven was vastly different when he described it to F. Scott Fitzgerald in a letter on July 1, 1925: "To me heaven would be a big bull ring with me holding two barrera seats and a trout stream outside that no one else was allowed to fish in and two lovely houses in the town;

Hemingway as a comic character in his high school yearbook, *Senior Tabula*, 1917.

Hemingway in a headline in a yearbook comic, *Senior Tabula,* 1917.

one where I would have my wife and children and be monogamous and love them truly and well and the other where I would have my nine beautiful mistresses on 9 different floors."

Finally, junior Al Dungan draws Hemingway singing his class off into the future: "Good bye those dear old high school days." Notably, the young Hemingway was not much of a singer, although he did play cello in his high school orchestra.

Detail of Hemingway in a yearbook comic in *Senior Tabula,* 1917.

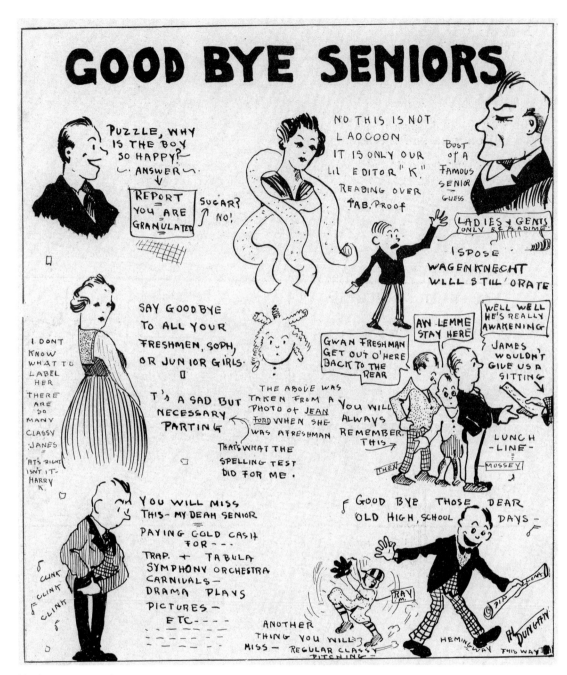

Hemingway as a comic character in a farewell page to seniors. *Senior Tabula*, 1917.

Captain Marvel Adventures #110 (July 1950)

Hemingway's first known appearance in mainstream comics was a bit underwhelming. In fact, you have to squint to see him. As Captain Marvel and President Harry Truman tour the Half-Century Fair of 1950, Hemingway is one of the luminaries who populates a panel of cultural leaders. He is in the upper left-hand corner, accompanied by contemporaries such as Walter Winchell, Albert Einstein, Bing Crosby, Jackie Robinson, and Louis B. Mayer.

Hemingway in *Captain Marvel Adventures* #110, 1950. © Fawcett Publications, Inc.

Coogy (1953)

This is the first of several Hemingway parody comics to appear in *Coogy*, Irving "Irv" Spector's *Pogo*-inspired strip syndicated by the *New York Herald-Tribune*.

The strip had a brief run, from 1951 to 1954, and Spector became better known for his "funny animal comics" and as an animator, notably on *The Jetsons* and *The Flintstones*. He also logged writing credits on *How the Grinch Stole Christmas* and Pink Panther cartoons.

Parody of two Hemingway novels in *Coogy*, 1953. © New York Herald-Tribune.

This Sunday strip, "Across the Old Man and into the Sea" parodies two Hemingway novels (*The Old Man and the Sea* and *Across the River and into the Trees*). In the story, Mo (a bear) is mistaken for a marlin and lashed to the side of an overzealous fisherman's dry-docked boat. Ultimately, Mo gets rescued by his grandson Coogy and a friend, as the manic fisherman is left to dream about a successful catch.

Mad Magazine #24 (1955)

"PAPPA" HEMINGHAW

Hemingway parody in *Mad Magazine #24*, 1955. © Pierce Publishing Corporation.

Hemingway is the subject of a parody in *Mad*'s first issue as a magazine, after its first 23 as a comic book. The author—here "Pappa" Heminghaw—finds himself in the jaws of a lion, as illustrated by Bernard "Bernie" Krigstein, who also provides the opening splash-page illustration. *Mad* parodies Hemingway's 1950 novel *Across the River and into the Trees* in text as *Out of the Frying Pan and into the Soup*, promoting it as "The First Part of a ½ Part Novel."

This issue of *Mad* came five years after E. B. White's skewering of the same novel in the *New Yorker*, with a parody titled "Across the Street and into the Grill." In all, the *Mad* parody seems oddly timed, coming three years after Hemingway's *The Old Man and the Sea*, which won the Pulitzer Prize and propelled him to win the Nobel Prize.

Frantic! #1 (1958)

Hemingway gets spoofed again in *Mad* knockoff *Frantic!* Cuban-born creator Ric Estrada was a Hemingway fan; he also did a story in *Our Army at War* #234 (see p. 17). In fact, Estrada often told of the impact Hemingway had on his life.

"In 1947, at the age of 19, I was sponsored by my journalist uncle Sergio Carbo and his friend Ernest Hemingway to move to New York and study art and become a professional cartoonist," Estrada wrote on his blog, before his death in 2009.

Here, three scant images illustrate a full page of text parodying *The Old Man and the Sea*. "Ernest Heminghay" is the author of "The Old Man and the She."

An 84-year-old man struggles to keep his young girlfriend away from "the sharks," aka Ivy League men with "three-button suits and crew cuts and filtered cigarettes."

"I caught her truly and well, and she is a good catch and she is mine," the old man says.

Facing page: "The Old Man and the She," Hemingway parody from *Frantic!*, 1958. © Pierce Publishing Corporation.

THE OLD MAN and the SHE

by Ernest Heminghay

He was an old man who lived alone in a skiff in the Gulf Stream and he had gone eighty-four years now without taking a wife. For the first fifty years he had had hope. But after fifty years without a wife the villagers said that the old man was now definitely and finally *jinxed*, which is the worst form of unlucky.

The old man was thin and gaunt with deep wrinkles in his wrinkles. Everything about him was old except his eyes and they were the same blue color as his blue jeans and were cheerful and undefeated and so were his jeans which hung together cheerful and undefeated even though they had been patched many times. But they had been truly patched so the old man still wore them. Besides, they were the only pair of pants he had. Truly.

Then one day the old man was not seen for a week. Then he came back and with him was a woman. She was truly a woman, a fine big one complete in every way and she had truly fine big ones and the old man was very proud.

The villagers watched the old man and the she as they walked through the village.

"See," they said. "He has the she."

"Si."

"Si, si."

26

"Si, si. I see the she."

Then, passing the Terrace, the old man sighed.

"Ay," he said. "Galanos. Sharks."

The sharks were not truly sharks. That was just the name given the young men who lounged on the Terrace, with their three-button suits and crew cuts and filtered cigarettes. They were *muchos Ivy League* and they sat on the Terrace all day drinking martinis *con* lemon peel and whistling at the girls. Often after the whistling one of the *Galanos* would walk off with one or more of the girls or one of the girls would walk off with one or more of *Galanos*. And the old man had a fear in him that this would happen now.

"Ay," he said. "I caught her truly and well, and she is a good catch and she is mine. I will not give her up. She is a big one and I will fight the *Galanos* to keep her."

But already the *Galanos* were whistling and she turned her head to them. The old man put out his hand but his hand was trembling.

"What would the great DiMaggio do in a situation like this?" he said. "But I am not the great DiMaggio. I am good field, no hit. All my life it has been this way. I have the understanding but I have not the strength and skills."

The woman was silent and the old man had hope. Then she turned away and the old man knew it was no use. He had caught her truly and well but now he had lost. She was walking away, going off with the *Galanos*, the sharks. He knew he was alone and would never see her again.

The old man walked to his skiff. The boy was waiting for him. The old man had taught the boy to whistle Dixie and the boy loved him.

"I saw," the boy said.

"Yes," the old man said.

"She was a fine big one," the boy said.

"Yes."

"But she got away."

"Yes."

"Even so, your luck has changed."

"No."

"Tell me, old man. Who was the lady."

"She was no lady," the old man said. "She was my wife."

The boy was silent. Then he said, "Ay. Si. The *Galanos*."

"It is so," the old man said,

"Yes."

"No."

"No."

"Yes."

"Rest," the boy said. "I will bring a beer."

The old man nodded and the boy went away. The boy was crying.

The old man rested. But he did not rest truly and well. He lay back and slept, dreaming of the big one that had got away. She was a fine big one and he had caught her but she had got truly away.

Le Journal de Tintin #586 (1960)

This short breakout story in France's *Tintin* features a five-page Hemingway story by the Belgian team of writer Yves Duval and artist Edouard Aidans.

Introduced to the *Kansas City Star* by his uncle and interviewed by its editor in chief, Hemingway justifies his passion for journalism by saying he wants to "experience the big/meaningful events before relaying them to the audience." To do so, however, he first has to convince the editor to let him tackle more important tasks than just "recording incoming phone calls."

Thankfully, the opportunity presents itself when Hemingway receives a call informing him of a street fight in progress. He quickly decides to cover the event and arrives on the scene at the same time as the emergency services by heroically jumping onto a moving ambulance. This starts a series of successful yet dangerous reports, from covering the Italian front during World War I to shooting a rhinoceros in Africa. "Living a peaceful life is unimaginable for this daredevil!"

The story was reprinted in black and white in 2003's *Les Meilleurs Recits de Aidans et Duval* #8 (*The Best Stories of Aidans and Duval*), printed by Franco-Belgian publisher Loup.

Hemingway story in *Le Journal de Tintin* #586, 1960.

Facing page: Hemingway in *Les Meilleurs Recits de Aidans et Duval* #8, 2003.

Hemingway's Superheroes

Sharon Hamilton

One of Hemingway's superheroes, Mordecai "Three Fingered" Brown, Chicago Cubs, baseball card portrait, 1909–11. American Tobacco Company. Benjamin K. Edwards Collection. Library of Congress, Prints and Photographs Division, reproduction number, LC-DIG-bbc-0713f.

Hemingway grew up before the invention of comic book superheroes. Superman did not make his red-caped and blue-tighted way into American popular culture until 1938, long after Hemingway's birth in 1899. But Hemingway knew the joy of illustrated superheroes nonetheless.

In Hemingway's case, those illustrated "action pictures" were of the American baseball stars who dominated the popular culture of his time. Baseball cards first appeared in the 1880s, still the early days of photography. Since the baseball players who appeared on those cards had to hold their poses in faked studio action shots, with baseballs suspended on strings, the resulting photographs unsurprisingly lack the dynamism of the sport.

To address this issue, hand-drawn images of baseball players also began to appear. During Hemingway's youth, illustrated images of the game's superheroes included New York Giants pitcher Christopher "Christy" Mathewson and Chicago Cubs pitcher Mordecai "Three Fingered" Brown.

Mathewson and Brown were real-life heroes. Both were later inducted into the Baseball Hall of Fame. The popular images of such players formed as much a part of Hemingway's childhood as comic books would for subsequent generations. These were Hemingway's superheroes.

Later, Hemingway's novels would reveal just how much of Mathewson and Brown's philosophies regarding what it means to be truly great infused his early imagination. For example, you get a hint of what became the famous "Hemingway code," with its emphasis on "grace under pressure," in Mathewson's popular 1912 book *Pitching in a Pinch,* which Hemingway is very likely to have read.

As Mathewson wrote, "In most Big League ball games, there comes an inning on which hangs victory or defeat. Certain intellectual fans call it the crisis; college professors, interested in the sport, have named it the psychological moment; Big League managers mention it as the 'break,' and pitchers speak of the 'pinch.' This is the time when each team is straining every nerve either to win or to prevent defeat."

In this moment, Mathewson explained, "the players and spectators realize that the outcome of the inning is of vital importance. And in most of these pinches, the real burden falls on the pitcher. It is at this moment that he is 'putting all he has' on the ball, and simultaneously his opponents are doing everything they can to disconcert him."

You get a sense, too, of the kind of heroism Hemingway found in his baseball superheroes through Mathewson's description of one of Hemingway's favorite players, Chicago Cubs pitcher Three Fingered Brown. Of Brown, who lost part of a finger in a childhood farm accident, Mathewson wrote: "Brown is my idea of the almost perfect pitcher. He is always ready to work. It is customary for most managers in the Big Leagues to say to a man on the day he is slated to pitch: 'Well, how do you feel to-day? Want to work?' Then if the twirler is not right, he has a chance to say so. But Brown always replies: 'Yes, I'm ready.'" In general, Mathewson observes, "It will usually be found at the end of a season that he has taken part in more games than any other pitcher in the country."[1]

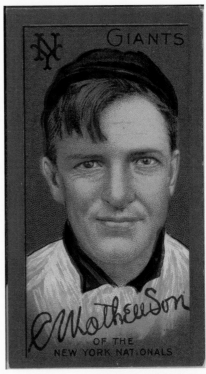

Christopher "Christy" Mathewson, one of Hemingway's superheroes.

We know that Hemingway admired both of these real-life heroes. Later, he would embody their spirit in the character of Santiago in *Old Man and the Sea,* who is determined, like Three Fingered Brown, to work hard so he will be ready for when luck comes and, like Mathewson, to be willing to face physical and psychological moments of crisis.

In 1912 (the year he turned 13) Hemingway responded to an advertisement in *Sporting News* magazine for baseball "action pictures." To Mr. Charles C. Spink and Son, Hemingway wrote, "Enclosed find $.35 for which send me [*sic*] the following baseball action pictures." Hemingway requested images of Mathewson and Brown, along with several other players, before signing off, "Yours Truly, Ernest Hemingway."[2]

As a boy, Hemingway found inspiration in the exploits of amazing illustrated action figures who dominated the mass media of his time. Later, in a plot twist worthy of his own novels, he would become a larger-than-life illustrated action figure—fighting alongside Wolverine and matching wits with Superman. The illustrated baseball action figures of Hemingway's youth existed at the beginning of his life story. Later, both he and his work would be transformed into drawings—and would thus enter the realm of myth.

Notes

1. Christy Mathewson, *Pitching in a Pinch and Other Baseball Stories "From the Inside"* (1913; repr., Newhall, CA: Matthewson Foundation, 2018, Kindle).

2. Hemingway to Charles C. Spink and Son [c. 1912], *The Letters of Ernest Hemingway,* vol. 1 of 4, *1907–1922,* ed. Sandra Spanier and Robert W. Trogdon (New York: Cambridge Univ. Press, 2011), 11.

1961–1990

Hemingway's Suicide and Early Guest Appearances

Vidas Ilustres: Ernest Hemingway (1964)

What the 1964 Mexican comic book *Illustrious Lives* gets wrong with the facts it makes up for in emotion. These 32 pages of adoring, biography-bending passion begin with the legend and work backward. The most harmless example: Hemingway grows a beard at age 18 and never shaves it.

Particularly interesting: the final page of Hemingway's bloodless suicide, where he's discovered not by his wife Mary but by a young man who says, "Pronto! Un Medico!" The next caption translates as, "It is believed that his death was an accident that happened as he cleaned his shotgun."

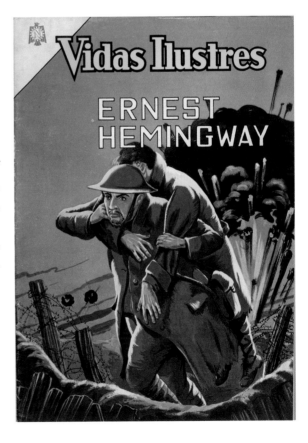

Hemingway biography attempt in comic book *Vidas Ilustres.*

Our Army at War #234 (July 1971)

In this Sergeant Rock–led book, Ernest Hemingway, F. Scott Fitzgerald, and John Dos Passos appear in a backup story titled "Mercy Brigade." In the eight-page story, a (historically inaccurate) blond Ernie rescues hospital patrons during a bombing raid, providing cover with a table he carries on his back, saying, "Don't despair! Old Ernie's here!" He also foils an espionage plot and inadvertently kills the knife-wielding villain with a single punch.

"I–I've killed a man, I killed a man," he says, before his friends divert him back to the battle at hand.

In his synopsis of the book, writer-illustrator Ric Estrada provides more context about the story: "This was a highly fictionalized account of three young men who served in the ambulance corps during World War I . . . who went on to become famous authors: Hemingway, Fitzgerald and John Dos Passos."

How highly fictionalized? Fitzgerald never left the United States during World War I. Perhaps Estrada could have included Walt Disney, who served with the Red Cross in France, in the tale.

A blond yet heroic Hemingway in *Our Army at War* #234, 1971. © DC Comics.

Corto Maltese: Celtic Tales (1972)

In Hugo Pratt's story "Under the Flag of Gold," a Hemingway stand-in, Officer Hernestway, helps liberate gold hidden by the king of Montenegro in the church of Sette Casoni. Hernestway only shows up in a few panels, as a volunteer ambulance driver for the American Red Cross, the same job Hemingway held in Italy before he was injured in a mortar attack on the Italian front.

Pratt's title character, Corto Maltese, also appears in Chris Hunt's Hemingway-inspired *Carver* series (2015) as an unnamed sailor (see pp. 189–197, this volume).

Bottom left: Hemingway as Officer Hernestway in *Corto Maltese: Celtic Tales,* 1972. © Casterman.

Bottom right: Ernest Hemingway as an American Red Cross volunteer during World War I, Milan, Italy. Ernest Hemingway Collection. John F. Kennedy Presidential Library and Museum, Boston.

Superman #277 (1974)

Writer Elliot S! Maggin has fun with a Norman Mailer / Ernest Hemingway mash-up character dubbed Ted "Pappy" Mailerway, a reporter-turned-hunter and a temperamental man of adventure.

"At the time I wrote that story I was going through a long-term Hemingway jag. And my friend Denny O'Neil was doing a similar Mailer binge. I had always thought of Mailer as a kind of rogue not quite worthy of Hemingway-esque hero worship. I thought of Hemingway as a more productive rogue," Maggin said.

He continued: "I had a professor who was a friend of Mailer and that made him seem a much smaller figure to me, I guess. But I had a lot of respect for Denny's perceptiveness, so I was re-evaluating Mailer in my mind and

Hemingway mash-up character in *Superman* #277, 1974. © DC Comics.

Ted "Pappy" Mailerway in *Superman* #277, 1974.

ended up merging him with Hemingway for that character. Maybe I was just sucking up to Denny. Who knows?"

In the story, Mailerway is a reporter at the *Daily Planet,* before the arrival of Clark Kent. He put the moves on Lois Lane, and in one flashback panel, he embraces her from behind and suggests they cover a story together abroad.

"N-no, thanks, Mr. Mailerway! I'm just a city girl!" she tells him.

Curt Swan provided pencils on "The Biggest Game in Town!" in which Mailerway hunts the biggest game in Metropolis: Superman. He doesn't want to kill the Man of Steel, mind you, just prove that he's Clark Kent. In the end, Superman outwits Mailerway, who still has his doubts about the last son of Krypton's secret identity.

"The Short Happy Life of Francis Macomber" (1975)

This crisp, faithful adaptation by Imre Sebock appeared in *Füles,* a Hungarian crossword magazine. Between word clues, readers could follow the marital strife and safari adventure that doesn't end well for man or beast.

Hungarian version of Hemingway's Francis Macomber story.

Facing page: An adaptation of Hemingway's short story "The Short Happy Life of Francis Macomber," as published in a 1975 issue of *Füles,* a Hungarian crossword magazine.

FRANCIS MACOMBER RÖVID BOLDOGSÁGA

12. MACOMBER NYOMORULTUL ÉRZI MAGÁT. A FÉLELEM MÉG MINDIG OTT TÁTONG, MINT VALAMI HIDEG, NYÁLKÁS ÜREG, ABBAN A NAGY SEMMIBEN, AHOL VALAMIKOR AZ ÖNBIZALMA FÉSZKELT, ÉS ETTŐL A ROSSZULLÉT KÖRNYÉKEZI.

MEGFUTOTTAM, MINT EGY NYÚL.

ELÉG! NE BESZÉLJÜNK TÖBBET AZ OROSZLÁNRÓL!

MAJD HELYREÜTI A CSORBÁT HOLNAP. BIVALYRA MEGYÜNK.

13. ÉN IS MEGYEK.

A MEMSAHIB NEM JÖHET VELÜNK.

14. MEGYEK! KÜLÖNBEN IS ROPPANT SZERETNÉM ÚJRA LÁTNI MAGÁT A MUNKÁJA KÖZBEN. ISTENI VOLT MA REGGEL. MÁR AMENNYIRE ÁLLATOK FEJÉT SZÉJJELLÖVÖLDÖZNI ISTENI.

„ELJÖTT AZ ÉN ÓRÁM" – GONDOLJA WILSON. ISMERI ÜGYFELEIT. A NEMZETKÖZI ÚRI VADÁSZTÁRSASÁGOK TAGJAINAK RENDEZ SAFARIKAT, AHOL A NŐK ÚGY ÉRZIK, NEM KAPTÁK MEG A PÉNZÜK ELLENÉRTÉKÉT, HA NEM BÚJNAK BE A FEHÉR VADÁSZ ÁGYÁBA. MEGVETI ŐKET, DE HÁT BELŐLÜK ÉL; AZ ERKÖLCSÜK AZ Ő ERKÖLCSE.

15. MACOMBERT A BENYAKALT SOK CITROMOS WHISKY HAMAR ELALTATJA. HAJNALTÁJT AZONBAN FELRIAD, ÉS ÉSZREVESZI, HOGY A FELESÉGE NINCS MELLETTE. EBBEN A TUDATBAN VIRRASZT KÉT ÓRÁN ÁT. VÉGRE...

HOL VOLTÁL?

16. HELLÓ! MÉG FENT VAGY? KIMENTEM LEVEGŐZNI.

ÍGY IS LEHET MONDANI. TE RINGYÓ!

TE PEDIG PIPOGYA FRÁTER VAGY! DE KÉRLEK, DRÁGÁM, NE VESZEKEDJÜNK MOST, NAGYON ÁLMOS VAGYOK. JÓ ÉJT!

Weird War Tales #68 (1978)

Hemingway—uncharacteristically smoking a pipe and clad in a reporter's trench coat and fedora—stars in *The Greatest Story Never Told,* a six-page tale by Paul Kupperberg, with pencils by a young Frank Miller, who would later find fame with *The Dark Knight Returns* (1986) and *Sin City* (1991), among other titles.

Kupperberg remembers: "I had no idea who was going to draw it when I wrote it, and even if the editor had told me it was going to be Frank Miller, I would have asked, 'Who?' Frank was still a total newbie at the time, with only a couple of short stories to his credit."

In a story set in 1937, Hemingway covers the Spanish Civil War near the city of Teruel, a Nationalist stronghold. Instead of a battle, he finds himself witnessing townsfolk summoning a demon to wipe out 100 Fascist soldiers.

After the otherworldly massacre, Hemingway is spotted by an old man, whom he tells: "I have always felt an affinity for the underdog with the courage to bite back! And you, mi amigo, have style—and the rarest of gifts of a people at war . . . grace under pressure."

Fitting the theme of the series, Hemingway says, "One has to expect horrors in war—of all sorts! This is merely one of a different kind."

Kupperberg likes using historical figures in stories; Alexander Graham Bell pops up in one of his *Atom* stories. In 1978, Kupperberg was only a year or two removed from having earned his college degree in English literature, which influenced his choice of characters.

"I'd been reading a lot of Hemingway and Fitzgerald . . . so I guess when I was trying to come up with ideas for *Weird War Tales,* Hemingway's time as a correspondent during the Spanish Civil War was on my mind," Kupperberg says.

Though not a fan of the hypermasculine Hemingway persona, Kupperberg says Papa "had a lasting impact on me stylistically. . . . His prose was

Hemingway in *Weird War Tales* #68, 1978. © DC Comics.

sharp enough to cut and I love his spare, clean style, especially by the time he got to *The Old Man and the Sea*. To this day I use a lot of little stylistic tics that I picked up reading him."

Kupperberg's story got a second life 11 years later, when it was reprinted in *Sgt. Rock Special #6*.

Doonesbury (Sunday, April 5, 1981)

The opening quotation from Hemingway to F. Scott Fitzgerald is comedically apocryphal, but the Hemingway letter *Doonesbury* creator Garry Trudeau references is real.

In May 1950, Hemingway wrote to literary critic Arthur Mizener: "I remember [author Ford Madox Ford] telling me that a man should always write a letter thinking how it would read to posterity. That made such a bad impression that I burned every letter in the flat including Ford's. . . . I write letters because it is fun to get letters back. But not for posterity. What the hell is posterity anyway?"

Although Trudeau doesn't remember where he ran across the quotation, it comes from a period when he was immersing himself in great American novels he'd missed in school. "I started with Fitzgerald, and this must have been during the Hemingway period that followed," says Trudeau.

Part of the cartoonist's affinity for Hemingway comes from his use of language. "I was very impressed with how much he was able to do with so little," Trudeau says. "[Mark] Twain said that the difference between the almost right word and the right word was the difference between the lightning bug and the lightning. Given the narrow range of his word choices, it was astonishing how much lightning flashed through Hemingway's work. The spare language, of course, has famously lent itself to parody, but for a strip cartoonist, his work was a master class in economy and precision. The main difference in my writing now from when I began is I use fewer words. I kill a lot of lightning bugs."

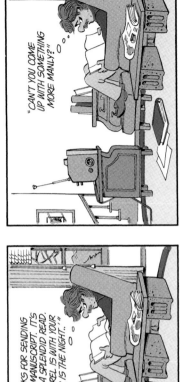

DOONESBURY
by GB Trudeau.

"SCOTTY, THANKS FOR SENDING ON YOUR NEW MANUSCRIPT. IT'S A FINE BOOK. A SPLENDID READ. MY ONLY QUARREL IS WITH YOUR TITLE, 'TENDER IS THE NIGHT'..."

"CAN'T YOU COME UP WITH SOMETHING MORE MANLY?"

I know it's been a while since you've heard from me, but I've recently been reading the letters of Ernest Hemingway for an American literature course and I got inspired.

Hemingway said the only reason he wrote letters was to get letters back, but I think there are other reasons. In an age of instant communication, writing offers an opportunity to collect one's thoughts.

Dear Dad,
Hold on to your pacemaker, it's an actual letter —it's an actual letter from your son...

Life here at school proceeds apace. Yesterday I had a small mishap with my motorcycle that resulted in a $300 repair bill. If you could help me out here, I promise to repay you at the end of the summer.

Too infrequently we take the time to shrug off our indolence and give expression to our feelings in any thoughtful and coherent fashion. This letter is a first, modest effort at personal reform.

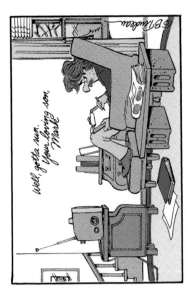

Well, gotta run.
Your loving son,
Mark.

Adventures of Uncle Scrooge Treasury #3: Der Ausflug nach Key West (The Trip to Key West) (1984)

Papa gets Disney-fied in this tale of Donald Duck and family searching for treasure in Key West as a hurricane looms off the Florida coast.

I saw a few warped panels from this comic framed on the walls of Hemingway's house in Key West. The word balloons were in German, and I couldn't find a version in English. I was stumped until Klaus Strzyz, a former editor and translator for Ehapa Verlag (the publisher of Disney comics in Germany), pointed me to this 1984 comic book.

The Disney comics database maintained by Inducks.org identifies Miquel Pujol as the artist and author of the story, with input by Adolf Kabatek, then chief editor of Ehapa Verlag. In a private letter to Strzyz, however, Kabatek calls this work "my third story. I myself think that I really have done a good job here." Pujol, via Inducks, credits Kabatek's contribution as more the work of an editor who could alter endings and had final say in the story but who also suggested the setting.

In this panel, Papa chats with a friend outside of Sloppy Joe's Bar in 1935, as the town braces for the hurricane. It's worth noting that the real Hemingway weathered a hurricane that same year, which inspired his piece "Who Murdered the Vets?"—his firsthand account of the storm, published in *New Masses*.

The author is the older, beard-and-sweater Karsh version of Hemingway, as all time collapses and is boiled down to the iconic. In another panel, this Hemingway carries a copy of *The Old Man and the Sea*, which he would start writing in 1951 in Cuba—16 years after this story. Donald Duck and his nephews also run into Papa in front of the modern-day Sloppy Joe's Bar at 201 Duval Street in Key West—not the 1935 location down the street, in what is now Captain Tony's Saloon at 428 Greene Street.

Sloppy Joe's Bar and Hemingway in panels from *Adventure of Uncle Scrooge Treasury #3*, 1984. © Ehapa Verlag.

Above: The modern Sloppy Joe's Bar—home of the annual Hemingway Look-Alike competition—which moved to its current location in 1937. Photo by Robert K. Elder, 2019.

Right: Captain Tony's Saloon at 428 Greene Street, which Hemingway knew as Sloppy Joe's Bar in 1935. Singer-songwriter Jimmy Buffet would later get his start here. Photo by Robert K. Elder, 2019.

Peanuts (Tuesday, August 28, 1984)

Peanuts creator Charles Schulz had several Hemingway books in his personal library, including hardback copies of *For Whom the Bell Tolls* (1940) and Mary Hemingway's *How It Was* (1976). Schulz even had a softcover version of Lillian Ross's *Portrait of Hemingway,* published by the Modern Library in 1999. However, in the whole *Peanuts* catalog, Hemingway's name appears only in this strip.

Schulz was much more of an F. Scott Fitzgerald fan, partially because both were natives of St. Paul, Minnesota. References to *The Great Gatsby* and Fitzgerald appear more than a dozen times in *Peanuts.*

Like Hemingway, however, Schulz thought word choice was paramount. In 1957, the *Saturday Evening Post* wrote, "Schulz is an inveterate fusser over the words he uses in the dialogue he puts into the mouths of his babes. While he will yield to editorial supervision from the syndicate on matters involving commas and dashes, he regards himself as a precisionist in the selection of words. It is a subject on which he stands his ground. 'Nobody tells Hemingway [what words to use],' says Schulz."

World's Finest Comics #304 (1984)

Hemingway, looking like the Comedian from Alan Moore's *Watchmen,* makes a cameo in the backstory of the superhero villain duo Null and Void. Writer David Anthony Kraft features the Crooks Company, a reference to the Crook Factory, a real-life covert submarine-hunting and spy ring in Cuba that Hemingway headed up during World War II. His third wife, Martha Gellhorn, later called the operation an excuse to drink with his friends and to get more gas for fishing trips, while allowing Papa to play soldier.

In 2009, Terry Mort published an entire book about the subject, *The Hemingway Patrols: Ernest Hemingway and His Hunt for U-Boats.* "Hemingway was the only American civilian to patrol off of Cuba," Mort told the Daily Beast website. "But he was part of a huge surveillance network in place. You just never knew when the subs were going to come up.

When ships in the Hooligan Navy spotted U-boats, they'd call for backup from the military."

But Hemingway had other things in mind, Mort said. "If he spotted a U-boat, not only would he call for backup, he wanted to attack the sub himself. So he took some hand grenades and Thompson machine guns with him on his boat. Of course, trying to attack one of the subs was suicidal. . . . His experience hunting U-boats was a perfect metaphor for how he saw the universe: as something unpredictable, impersonal and lethal."

Hemingway in *World's Finest Comics* #304, 1984.
© DC Comics.

1991–2000

Hemingway Goes Meta—
Time Travel and Hero Worship

WildC.A.T.s Covert Action Teams
#41 and #42 (1992)

Why is the young Hemingway sometimes (erroneously) fair-haired in the comics? In this time-travel story, the WildC.A.T.s chase their adversaries—the Puritans—across history to keep them from altering it. In these issues, Grifter, Void, Max Cash, and company find themselves in World War I, aided by a teen-aged Hemingway, who drives them around in his Red Cross ambulance.

Across two issues, the creators manage to mis-spell Ernest (as "Earnest") and Hemingway (as "Hemmingway") and put him on the French instead of the Italian front, but time travel challenges many storytelling conventions, so why not spelling and geography?

Hemingway in *WildC.A.T.s Covert Action Teams*, 1992. © Image Comics.

Wolverine #35–37 (1991)

When a time vortex takes Wolverine back to the Spanish Civil War, he encounters Hemingway at a bullfight and promptly takes a swig from the author's wine bottle. Heroic Hemingway acts as a guide to the out-of-time Wolverine and fellow Canadian superhero Puck. Papa, however, is a secondary character in this three-issue arc, barely appearing in the same panels with Wolverine until the very last frame.

"I always liked Hemingway," says writer Larry Hama. "Wish I could write as pared-down as him, but that requires real bravery."

George Orwell also appears in this story under his real name, Eric Arthur Blair, in a story inspired by military historian Antony Beevor's *The Spanish Civil War*.

"It seemed like an interesting period for a time-travel story," Hama says. "I saw Picasso's painting [*Guernica*] when it was on loan to MOMA and it imprinted on me."

Hama employed his passion for detail by setting one of the major conflicts in the story in a mountain pass named Eroica. "It's historically accurate," Hama says. "The Republicans named passes after Beethoven works."

He continues: "Overall, it's not very accurate historically—especially the timeline concerning *Guernica*—but I did provide the artist [Marc Silvestri] with references for correct uniforms, aircraft and markings."

Hemingway in *Wolverine* #37, 1991. © Marvel Comics.

Sartre and Hemingway (1992)

What happens when a young, philosophical mind (Jean-Paul Sartre) meets a brawny, testosterone-soaked writer (Hemingway) in 1924's Paris? Answer: Hemingway fights a sword-wielding Salvador Dalí. Written and illustrated by Dick Matena, this hard-boiled tale revolves around Eva, Sartre's childhood love who was once a maid in his family's home and has now fallen into prostitution. Hemingway shows up to punch people.

"I liked Hemingway—still do—I loved to read about American writers in Paris," says Matena. "And I loathed Sartre. Still do."

Matena remembers writing the story quickly and liking the narrative, although he wasn't pleased with the artwork. That's why he republished the graphic novel in 2010 in black and white under the title *Paris 25/44.*

"[Hemingway was a] great writer, great artist, a brave man, very misunderstood and interpreted wrong as a human being during his lifetime," Matena says. "He was a very tormented person, driven to paranoia by several despicable witch-hunters."

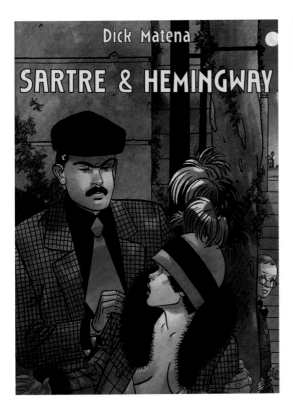

Left: Sartre & Hemingway, 1992. © Arboris Verlag.

Right: The cover of a black-and-white graphic novel featuring Hemingway, *Paris 25/44.*

This story, "A Movable Beast," is a play on words referring to Hemingway's posthumously published Paris memoir, *A Moveable Feast.*

Paris isn't the backdrop for this tale, however. It's set on an alien planet where Hemingway—clad in safari gear—finds himself hunted by the planet's reptilian inhabitants.

"I had in mind the 'Bad Hemingway' contest held every year to see who does the worst Hemingway-type writing," says writer Mike Baron. "And that's what I was shooting for in the story."

This story was part of Baron's *Feud* tales within *Heavy Hitters,* as published by Epic.

Artist Mark A. Nelson adds, "Since the story had a little tongue in cheek to it also, I pushed the *Great White Hunter* image and then pushed it a little further."

In short: things do not end well for Papa Hemingway.

"Hemingway was required reading when I was in school, so I read a lot of books and short stories," Nelson says. "His writing is terse and to the point, and there were always strong characters. I do enjoy that about his work."

Nelson continues: "My part was to deliver the visuals. The whole story is about the contrast of an alien world and Papa dropped in it. So, you have the great terse Hemingway character against the various reptilian creatures with their great Mike Baron words."

Hemingway in "A Movable Beast."

Hemingway: Muerte de un Leopardo (1993)

Hemingway is the focus of a revenge plot that spans decades in Marc Males and Jean Dufaux's *Hemingway: Death of a Leopard*. The story is broken into flashbacks in 1930s Africa and 1959 Cuba, where the author encounters the beautiful but complicated Anjelica, the daughter of two friends who died in Africa.

Anjelica blames Hemingway for her parents' deaths and then seduces him over dinner. "Writing for me will always be a good way of exorcising the past," Hemingway says in the story. Eventually, Fidel Castro's regime intervenes, and the conspiracy to kill Hemingway comes to a dramatic conclusion.

A Fidel Castro–like character in *Hemingway: Muerte de un Leopardo*, 1993. © Glenat.

Shade the Changing Man #31 and #32 (1993)

"What inspired me to put Hemingway in the book? Partly, because *Shade*—being a pretty crazy book where almost anything could happen—was a great opportunity to include two of my heroes: Hemingway and James Joyce," says writer Peter Milligan. "Both of these writers have meant an awful lot to me."

In this time-bending, two-issue story, Hemingway and Joyce team up with Shade to battle an adversary in the Area of Madness. In the 1990s, Milligan rebooted Steve Ditko's interdimensional adventurer, reimagining him as a postmodern hero intent on saving Earth from encroaching forces of madness. In one arc, Shade meets Hemingway and Joyce as time starts to become unstable.

"When I was young, I really responded to [Hemingway's] writing—especially his short stories. I loved that sense of so much meaning being hidden beneath the often simple actions of a short story. 'Cat in the Rain' and 'The End of Something' are two great examples of this," Milligan says.

Hemingway was obsessed with Joyce, who was 17 years his senior—although in *Shade* they are depicted as contemporaries. As mentioned in Hemingway's *New York Times* obituary, he wrote in a 1922 letter to Sherwood Anderson that a nearly blind Joyce once picked a fight, then stepped behind him and ordered: "Deal with him, Hemingway!" Milligan recreates and reimagines the scene and tucks in other bits of biography, notably Hemingway's early childhood dressed as a girl, when his mother raised him as the twin of his older sister.

In a particularly powerful part of this story, the two authors are transported from 1927 into a modern library—in which each gets to read his own biography. Hemingway doesn't like what he sees. Milligan's caption reads: "Hemingway moans audibly as he sees a photograph of himself taken only days before he committed suicide. . . . A withered white-haired man, old before his time, alcoholic and finished."

An event from Hemingway's life inspired this scene in *Shade the Changing Man,* 1993. © DC Comics.

Hemingway in *Shade the Changing Man,* 1993. © DC Comics.

Artist Colleen Doran had pneumonia while she was working on the story, and, as she recalls, "it was a devil meeting the deadline. This was all pre-internet, so I got my references at the library. . . . I had to do a bit of reading up on the authors and try to get something of their character in the pictures."

Milligan remembers, "Reading about Hemingway and Joyce's relationship in Paris, I was struck by how, though obviously very different in character and artistic intent, these two apparently got along famously. . . . I hope that something of their characters and their relationship came out in that crazy comic book."

Speciale Nathan Never #4, "Fantasmi a Venezia" (Ghosts in Venice) (1994)

When the canals of Venice start to lose water and the wife a friend goes missing, Nathan Never is sent to investigate.

Part *Blade Runner,* part Sam Spade story, this popular Italian comic book blends elements of sci-fi with film noir. Never, a detective from the Alfa Agency, encounters Hemingway while drinking at an outdoor café. Once Papa sits down, he tells Never about Venice and dispenses advice on everything from drinking vodka to aging.

"If you haven't lived, getting old is a nightmare," Hemingway says. "Life is something extraordinary, it should be lived. You should try to experience all the emotions."

The story takes a turn for the surreal when Nick Adams (Hemingway's literary alter ego) shows up as a former "great traveler" who now lives in Venice. Adams and Papa reminisce about places that don't exist anymore.

Expanding the narrative frame, Never begins deconstructing his own life: "If I was a character in a novel, I would think that the novel wasn't written by one person, but by multiple authors who didn't speak to one another beforehand."

Cover of a *Nathan Never* issue where the titular character encounters Hemingway and later on Nick Adams.

Hemingway in *Speciale Nathan Never* #4, 1994. © Sergio Bonelli Editore.

Hemingway responds: "It's always like this in life. There's no single author. Otherwise, imagine how boring life would be."

Eventually, aliens and spaceships explain the water's disappearance from Venice.

"The inspiration for this Nathan Never adventure came during a visit to Venice, in the midst of the city's famous carnival. The mood of the city and the mystery of the masks struck me," remembers writer Antonio Serra. "And they mingled with the memory of a famous film by James Cameron, *The Abyss.*"

However, Hemingway and Nick Adams (drawn by artists Nando Esposito and Denisio Esposito) weren't in the first draft of the story. Instead, Hugo Pratt, the famous Italian comic book author, and his alter ego, Corto Maltese, were supposed to provide the exposition (see pp. 17–18, this volume).

"Pratt has always been very attached to Venice, and several of his characters' adventures take place in the lagoon city. But the adventures of Nathan Never are set in the distant future, and this implied that Pratt must have died and perhaps should appear in the adventure as a ghost," Serra says.

But Pratt was still alive at the time, and the managing director of Serra's publishing house, Decio Canzio, was a close friend of Pratt's and was worried that his appearance as a ghost might offend him. So Pratt and Corto Maltese needed to be replaced.

"Because of the content of the story, I needed this new character to be a creative person with an easily recognizable alter ego," Serra says. "So, right away, my mind rushed to Ernest Hemingway and Nick Adams. Hemingway visited Venice several times and was a frequent visitor to the famous Harry's Bar. So my choice was easy!"

Murder Can Be Fun #2 (1996)

John Marr's zine *Murder Can Be Fun* profiled those who met bloody ends, and in the 1990s, Slave Labor Graphics turned the series into its own comic book. In the second issue, illustrator Zander Cannon's summary of Papa's life lasts all of two pages and sticks mostly to the facts, if you ignore the panel that depicts him as a war correspondent with a *Star Wars* AT-AT walker in the background.

"I thought I was pretty cute at the time to put an AT-AT in the background of the Spanish Civil War panel," Cannon recalls. "Those kind of 'chicken fat' background details are something I love, but it's funny how dumb it seems in retrospect."

With two pages, Cannon had limited space, "So I just kind of honed in on his suicide and the elements of his art and life that foreshadowed it."

For reference, he found a few images of Hemingway at his local library.

"And I really mean a *few* images, because I ended up drawing him as basically 60-year-old Hemingway at every stage of his life. It's ridiculous, but it kind of fit the tone of the zine and of my art style, which was—to be charitable—more interpretive than realistic. This was all done by the seat of everyone's pants, so I fit right in."

Cannon only came into conflict with his publisher in fact-checking. "The editor on the book added some quotation marks in the narration at the end where I had said that the press incorrectly reported that Hemingway had put the gun in his mouth," he says. "It *was* incorrect, but he put that word in quotes. I was trying to make the point that Hemingway's personality was so melancholic that the press was ready to take wild, salacious guesses about his death, even though they were wrong. It probably came across as too subtle or narratively mushy, hence the edit."

One small bit of grisly fact-checking: When Hemingway committed suicide, he tripped both triggers of his shotgun—not just one barrel.

Also in this issue: Jayne Mansfield, Andy Warhol, Bob Crane, and Brandon Lee.

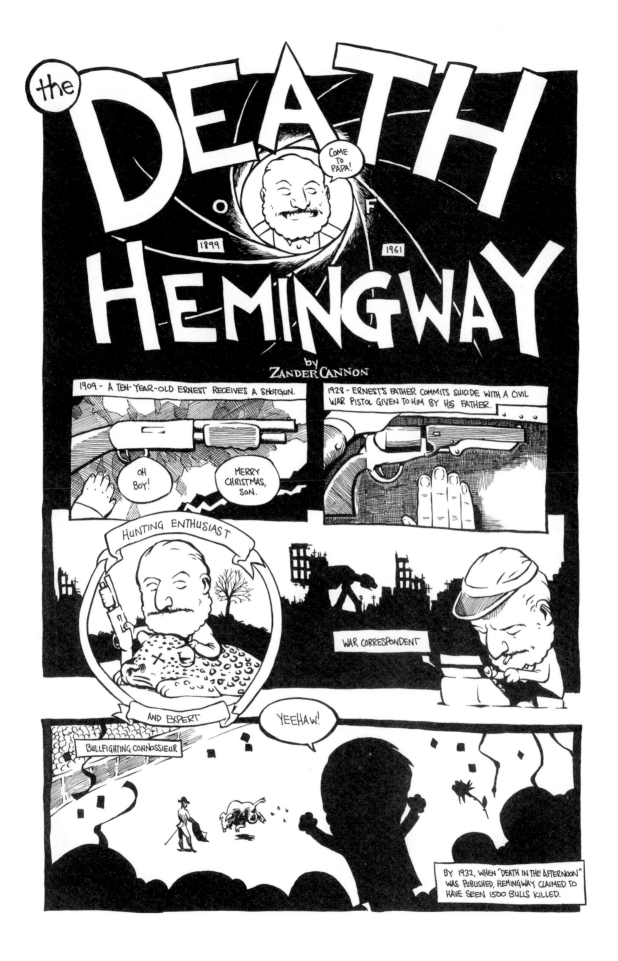

Samurai Crusader (1996–1998)

When pieces of this book ran as a series in the *Comics Journal,* reader Phil Rippke pointed out Hemingway's long-running appearance as the sidekick in *Samurai Crusader,* a manga series by writer Hiroi Oji and artist Ryoichi Ikegami (*Crying Freeman* and *Mai, the Psychic Girl*).

"The titular character is visiting Europe and meets the burly, two-fisted adventurer Hemingway and together they try to foil a plot to start a world war. Viz translated it into English and published a three-volume series from the '90s," Rippke writes. "It's definitely worth tracking down."

So, I did. There are three volumes:

Hemingway the sidekick in *Samurai Crusader,* 1996. © Viz Communications Inc.

- *Samurai Crusader: The Kumamaru Chronicles* (reprinting *Manga Vizion*, 1, nos. 1–8)
- *Samurai Crusader: Way of the Dragon* (reprinting *Manga Vizion*, 1, no. 8 through 2, no. 7)
- *Samurai Crusader: Sunrise over Shanghai* (1997, reprinting Manga Vizion, 2, no. 8 through 3, no. 5)

Rippke also directed me to Katherine Dacey's loving tribute to the series, published on the website Manga Bookshelf.

Dacey writes: "Whenever I see Ryoichi Ikegami's name attached to a project, I know two things: first, that the manga will be beautifully illustrated, and second, that the plot will be completely nuts. *Samurai Crusader,* a globe-trotting, name-dropping adventure from the early 1990s, provides an instructive example."

Lobo (second series) #36 (1997)

In Alan Grant's self-referential narrative, "Death Trek 100, Part Two: Analysis of a Story Where the Writer Runs Out of Plot," a pipe-smoking Hemingway appears as part of a literary Greek chorus. Accompanying him are Mark Twain, Geoffrey Chaucer, Herman Melville, William Shakespeare, and others.

Hemingway (with cats) in *Lobo,* 1997.

Artist Carl Critchlow wasn't supplied with any photo references, but the best he could manage in those pre-Google days were "some grainy images from my local reference library, where I also found mention of his love of cats—so I threw a few in to help with identification and kept my fingers crossed it was near enough for any interested parties to work out who it was supposed to be."

Lobo, of course, is on one of his ultra-violent rampages, as the famous authors add metacommentary. Example:

> Melville: "I don't understand, sir. . . . The story's finished, but there are three pages left to fill!"
> Shakespeare: "Oh, my God! I've just had a terrible thought—maybe he's filling it with us!"
> Hemingway: "You mean—we're only plot devices?"

Death by Chocolate (1997)

Time travel and talking dogs dominate David Yurkovich's wonderfully weird graphic novel.

"I wanted to do a time-travel story and feature Hemingway because I thought it would be an interesting challenge to insert him into the narrative. I can't say that the story was influenced by Clifford Simak's *City* (since at that time I wasn't even familiar with the work) but I'm fairly certain it was, at least subconsciously, influenced by Harlan Ellison's *A Boy and His Dog*," Yurkovich says.

Yurkovich's tales take place just prior to Hemingway's suicide, and this is foreshadowed, "though intentionally not graphically portrayed, toward the end of the story," he says.

At the heart of the story is Sir Geoffrey, a talking canine from another world on which dogs, not man, became the dominant species. Sir Geoffrey's society has begun to embrace the arts.

"Providing an artistic contribution to society is soon mandated by lawmakers, and Geoffrey is outcast for failing to possess any artistic skill. Seeking to leave his depressing existence, he teleports to Earth using a special ankle bracelet and is adopted by a caring family," Yurkovich says. "Geoffrey can read and write and eventually stumbles upon the works of Hemingway and is blown away by the writing. He decides to travel back in time and learn from Hemingway so that he can eventually return to his home world as a great writer."

Meanwhile, Sir Geoffrey is being hunted by the FBI and a mysterious trio safeguarding the time stream. Yurkovich also adds a chocolate car to the mix, if things weren't weird enough.

David Yurkovich (2019), graphic novel creator whose *Death by Chocolate* features Hemingway. Used with permission.

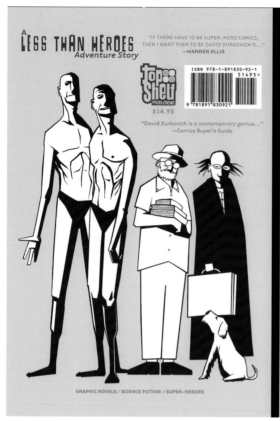

Above: Death by Choco-
late wraparound cover,
1997. David Yurkovich.
Used with permission.

Following pages: Death by
Chocolate, 1997.

"At that time I was trying to improve my drawing acumen, so I intentionally created scenes that would involve illustrating things I was not adept
at rendering (dogs, cats, classic cars, celebrities)," Yurkovich remembers.

In 2007, Top Shelf Productions published *Death by Chocolate: Redux* (a
collection of Yurkovich's earlier *Chocolate* comics along with new material). But why did he choose Hemingway for his tale?

"I think it's become fashionable to insert historic figures into comics.
I'm not quite sure when this trend first gained popularity, but I recall a
Sandman story by Neil Gaiman that featured Shakespeare," Yurkovich
says, noting that the tradition of celebrity cameos stretches over decades.
"Transitioning them from cameo to a supporting or central character
seems to have become popular around the time of *Watchmen*."

Today, Yurkovich says, it's fairly common to see authors and celebrities
playing major roles in comics stories.

"Hemingway is a seminal figure in literature and is internationally
known, so it seems logical that artists and writers would find inspiration
to feature him in works of sequential fiction," Yurkovich says.

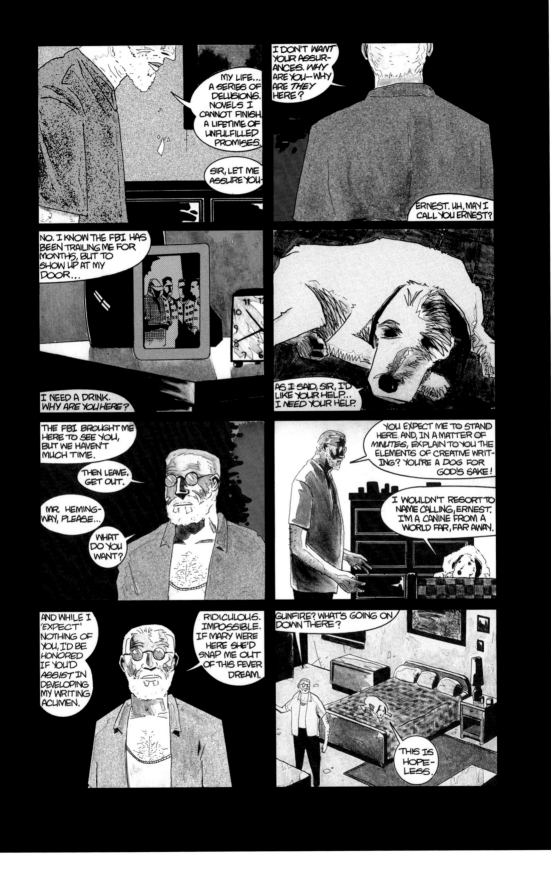

LISTEN POOCH, WHY SHOULD I HELP YOU?

WELL, YOU'D BE DOING ME A HUGE FAVOR, AND I'M A FAST LEARNER.

OH, REALLY?

WITH SWETE OUTSIDE, I SOON FOUND MYSELF SURROUNDED. I THOUGHT ABOUT MY NEXT MOVE...

OH YES, I ONCE TOOK A SWIMMING COURSE ON MY HOME PLANET. SIX YEARS LATER I COULD STILL DOGGY-PADDLE.

YES, BUT...

...WHEN AN INVISIBLE FORCE OF ENERGY RIPPED THE WEAPON FROM MY HAND.

WRITING AND SWIMMING ARE COMPLETELY SEPARATE DISCIPLINES. YOU CAN'T COMPARE THE TWO. WRITING IS BASED ON IMAGINATION, CREATIVITY, LIFE EXPERIENCE. IT'S ABOUT LIFE AND LOVE AND DEATH, TRAGEDY AND TRIUMPH. IT CAN'T BE REDUCED TO A SERIES OF ROBOTIC MOVEMENTS.

THE NUMBNESS IN MY HAND WAS OVERWHELMING.

THEY WALKED PAST ME, PAUSING BRIEFLY AT THE GUN.

BUT SURELY, WITH ALL OF YOUR ACCOMPLISHMENTS YOU COULD--

NO, I CAN'T.

I WAS POWERLESS TO STOP THEM. AS THEY ASCENDED THE STAIRS, I BEGAN TO WONDER HOW THINGS HAD GOTTEN THIS BAD.

Big Book of Vice (1998)

Strangely, Hemingway doesn't show up in the "Alcohol" chapter of Steve Vance's *Big Book of Vice*. Instead, he gets a one-panel cameo in the chapter on Cuba, illustrated by Rick Geary, as part of the "Sin Cities" section of the book.

The four-page "Fantasy Island" story was part of the *Big Book of Vice* anthology, which ran for 17 volumes in the DC / Paradox Press nonfiction Big Book series.

"All the stories in this volume were written by Steve Vance, and each one illustrated by a different artist," remembers artist Geary.

"For all the stories I did for the Big Books, I never had any contact with the writers. The editor just sent me the finished script, and I laid out the pages from that," Geary explains. "As for reference, these were the days before I had access to the internet, so I must have searched through library books and whatever other books I had on hand."

Nevertheless, Geary certainly captured Hemingway's smile and the paradoxes of Cuban society.

Jenny Sparks: The Secret History of the Authority #5 (2000)

Perhaps it's only natural that Hemingway—in this incarnation a trans-dimensional military officer—would be in love with Jenny Sparks, the living embodiment of the twentieth century from the pages of *The Authority*. During this incarnation, Sparks crisscrosses history, interacting with everyone from Adolf Hitler to John Lennon, for better or worse.

In this issue, Hemingway—who doubles as an international secret agent with futuristic weapons—saves Sparks from falling to her death and proposes marriage. He is rejected. "Oh, as if I'd be interested in anything other than becoming Mrs. Hemingway, you big Soppy Git," says Sparks.

Later, she gives him some literary advice: "I still say nobody's going to want to read a bloody novel called *The Old Cuban Guy and the Big Fish*."

Hemingway as a trans-dimensional military officer in *Jenny Sparks: The Secret History of the Authority* #5, 2000. © DC Comics.

Cerebus #251–65 (2000–2001)

In addition to Hemingway, other literary luminaries, or their doppelgängers, have appeared in Dave Sim's 300-issue run of *Cerebus*—among them Oscar Wilde, F. Scott Fitzgerald, and Gertrude Stein.

The title character—a humanoid aardvark who starts as a barbarian and becomes a prime minister, a pope, and, finally, an outcast—is the vehicle for Sim's exploration of philosophy, religion, and controversial gender politics.

In this story, "Form & Void," Cerebus treks home with his love, Jaka, and they encounter his idol, author "Ham Ernestway." This avatar depicts the author at the end of his life, nearly subverbal as he fights a losing battle with depression. His icy wife, Mary, always at his side, works to protect his legacy.

This spare story, appearing near the end of *Cerebus*'s run, is part comic book and part obsessive notebook of Sim's Hemingway-related citations and tangents published at the back of each issue. Sim goes to great lengths to prove that Mary Hemingway kept a handwritten journal from her 1953 African safari that has since been lost or destroyed in favor of her typed and edited manuscript. The arc's title "Form & Void" carries not only biblical connotations but also refers to Sim's self-described anti-feminist worldview, in which the (emotional) female void feeds off the (creative) male light. Gender politics—and gender fluidity—remain at the core of "Form & Void."

Sim's references rely heavily on Hemingway's posthumously published *The Garden of Eden* and its depiction of gender ambiguity. On one page in *Cerebus,* an older Hemingway begins to disrobe, revealing women's lingerie.

Hemingway is one of many literary figures to appear in *Cerebus,* but he does in the story "Form & Void."

Sim quotes Hemingway from a 1953 passage he wrote in Mary's diary: "Mary is a sort of prince of devils. . . . She always wanted to be a boy and thinks as a boy without ever losing any femininity. . . . She loves me to be her girl, which I love to be—not being absolutely stupid, and also loving to be her girl since I have other jobs in the daytime."

Sim goes farther than most scholars and biographers in claiming that Hemingway was bisexual. "If all of *The Garden of Eden* manuscript pages were ever published, I'm sure Hemingway would become a de facto bisexuality poster boy," he says.

Here, in an extended interview, Sim talks about Hemingway and *Cerebus.*

Q: What inspired you to put Hemingway in *Cerebus?*

Sim: I took Norman Mailer's word for it that Hemingway was the Undisputed Heavyweight Champion of the Literary World and decided that I would "do" him as the *capo di tutti capi* ["boss of all bosses"] literary presence

flip
flip

"Mary is a sort of prince of devils."

"She always wanted to be a boy and thinks as a boy without ever losing any femininity."

"If you should become confused on this you should retire."

Tic   TWITCH   FLINCH

CLENCH   SPASM

JERK   SLAM

"She loves me to be her girl, which I love to be — not being absolutely stupid, and also loving to be her girl since I have other jobs in the daytime."

TWITCH   TWITCH

in *Cerebus*—all without having read a word of his fiction. If he's good enough for Mailer, he's good enough for me.

Q: Did Hemingway's writing have any impact on your work?

Sim: I'm a huge fan of the very early Hemingway but ultimately decided that most of his work was "The Emperor's New Clothes." Not much "there" there. The lowercase *in our time* I would rate the highest [*in our time* was Hemingway's short story 1924 collection printed in Paris. His 1925 expanded edition, printed in New York, was uppercased as *In Our Time*]. Some parts of *Men without Women*. I'd rate Fitzgerald and Mailer higher than I do Hemingway.

Q: Even though you weren't a fan of Hemingway's work, what was your understanding of the author's popularity during his lifetime? What was his appeal?

Sim: The adventurer! All the frontiers would be explored in the course of Hemingway's lifetime and he was one of the last to travel to exotic locations and write about them, and his choices were very astute: He made Kilimanjaro, bullfighting, the running of the bulls at Pamplona, and the Spanish Civil War, among others, his own.

It must've been both a great joy and a great burden to be Hemingway, probably both simultaneously, and in a way that mixed very badly with atheism and alcohol. His "black ass" [moods were] largely self-inflicted, I think.

Q: Scholars have linked Hemingway's "black ass" moods, as Hemingway himself put it, to his family's generational struggle with clinical depression and a legacy of suicide. Since you wrote the "Form and Void" story arc, how have your views on mental illness changed?

Sim: They haven't. We all go through periods of "black ass" in our lives, and it's up to us to pull ourselves out of it. Hemingway didn't, which was a failure on his part. Period.

Q: In the endnote for "Form and Void" and in your essay "Tangent," you wrote that Mary Hemingway murdered her husband and should be brought up on "first degree murder" charges. It's been some time since you wrote that—was this hyperbole, or do you believe it to be true? Is the failure to prevent the last of several suicide attempts the same as committing murder?

Sim: The fact that she left the keys to the gun chest in plain sight suggests to me that she knew what she was doing and she knew what the result would be. So, it seems to me definitely premeditated. That having been said, it was Hemingway who unlocked the gun chest, loaded the weapon, and pulled the triggers.

Q: In 2012, you told *Comics Journal:* "I think Hemingway was completely bi-sexual," which is a bolder statement than his biographers have made. What you led to the conclusion that Hemingway was bisexual?

Sim: Two things: First, Mary Hemingway's Africa diary, where it was clear that he was fantasizing that she was a young boy—his "kitten

Facing page: Hemingway in *Cerebus*.

brother." . . . Second, *The Garden of Eden* book, which he wildly "over-wrote" to the tune of hundreds of pages trying to explain his sexuality in such a way as not to sound gay. He couldn't do it and gave up trying. If all of *The Garden of Eden* manuscript pages were ever published, I'm sure Hemingway would become a de facto bisexuality poster boy.

He wanted to be all man and all woman and he wanted his wives to be all man and all woman. Mary documented that in her journal, he snooped and read it and had to add his own entry after doing so, knowing that Mary's journal would be read, in order to "clarify" things for posterity. I think he thought that everyone was like that: all man and all woman and that he was the only one who was honest about it.

Above: Ernest and Mary Hemingway near huts while on safari in Africa, circa 1953–54. Ernest Hemingway Collection. John F. Kennedy Presidential Library and Museum, Boston.

Right: Hemingway in *Cerebus,* 2000. © Aardvark-Vanaheim, Inc. Reprinted with permission. All rights reserved.

A Conversation with *Cerebus* background artist Gerhard

In 2011, Sean Michael Robinson interviewed Dave Sim's collaborator, Gerhard, who had for decades provided the intricate background and noncharacter illustrations for *Cerebus*. He was instrumental in re-creating Hemingway's dual plane crashes in the series, although he had to invent what was essentially a medieval airship to mesh the worlds. In this excerpt, Gerhard talks with Robinson about the style and challenges of the sequence from issue 258, which is partially reprinted in this book. The full interview originally appeared on Comics Journal's website (TCJ.com) in a slightly different format.

Q: Tell me about the airship. It must have been enjoyable to design that.

Gerhard: Yeah. This sequence is based on the Hemingway stuff. He gave me the book that he was using for reference, with the stories of the two plane crashes. And we were both sort of like, "How the hell do we get airplanes into *Cerebus?*" And he knew my affinity for airplanes—I've always been into them, ever since I was a kid. It's been airplanes and drawing for me for as long as I can remember. So he set the task for me to design an airship that could exist in Cerebus's world. I knew because of the sound effects on 468 and 469 that it would have to be steam-powered. And obviously it would be a balloon, so the steam could provide hot air for the balloon.

And I've always been interested in boating too, ever since I started sailing, so it was a matter of combining those elements. So I've got a hot-air balloon and a boat that uses a big wing-like or duck-feet-like paddles that uses those to push itself through the sky. This was another thing that I made a computer model of. On 524, the sequence where it's circling the falls, is the actual sequence of how the paddles move. They go flat and straight for the forward motion so that there's the least amount of

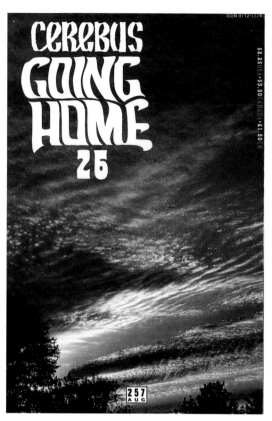

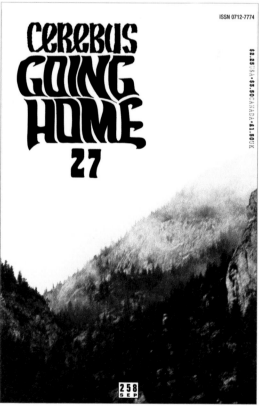

Top: Cerebus issue 257.

Right: Cerebus issue 258.

Above: Ernest Hemingway lying down, showing his injured hand and burnt stomach after his plane crash, circa 1953. Ernest Hemingway Collection. John F. Kennedy Presidential Library and Museum, Boston.

Following pages: Hemingway in *Cerebus,* 2000.

air resistance, and they turn so they grab as much air as possible, and then they swing back and push the airship forward. And I had all that on a computer model, a very simple one, just to make sure I had the sequence right, so this thing could kind of paddle its way through the sky. Then there's the big crash scene on 537—that was fun to do.

Q: You didn't research any early steps of flight?

Gerhard: No, this had to be something right out of left field, that only existed in *Cerebus*'s world. Because I'd been such a fan of airplanes and flight, I was already really aware of the early steps of flight. So it was more like, "How would I have done it?" I don't actually have to physically do it myself, but in theory anyway, how would I approach it?

Q: 537 is a really beautiful page.

Gerhard: That was from a photo reference. That was the actual falls in Africa that they crashed near.

Papa had told Roy that we would wait at the fire for him, so he stayed behind

...and watched the elephants

We went down slowly

The boat was privately chartered by Mr. Ian McAdam.

...seeing no elephants.

Roy came back with McAdam

...and we sent the boys up the hill to get Papa.

My trip down with the boys had moved the elephants back up

...and they were disputing his knoll with him

Topolino

Hemingway in Italy's Disney Comics (1987–2001)

Italy loves Hemingway; in particular, Disney's Italian comic book creators love Hemingway.

Since 1987, the comic digest *Topolino* (Mickey Mouse's name in Italy) has published more than 10 stories that feature Hemingway as a character or are based on one of the author's stories. In Italy, where he was wounded in World War I and set two novels and several short stories, his cult of personality was particularly strong in comics. Most of these *Topolino* stories have not been translated into English or published in the United States.

In 1999, *Topolino* #2278 celebrated Hemingway's hundredth birthday with *Per chi suona il campanello* (For Whom the Doorbell Rings), which puts Mickey and Hemingway in the same tale. "In our story, Mickey decides to give up his adventures around the world, but a journalist named Ernest rings his doorbell to interview him," says *Topolino*'s Davide Catenacci, who served as a series editor in 1999. "During the interview, Mickey understands that adventure is part of his life and immediately leaves with renewed enthusiasm. . . . We thought that Mickey and Ernest had the same love of adventure and curiosity for the world. So, one year later . . ."

In 2000, Italian comic artist Giorgio Cavazzano devised a project called "8 X 8 . . . 49" (a nod to the publication of Hemingway's *The Fifth Column and the First Forty-Nine Stories*); this challenged creators in the *Accademia Disney* to produce comics in *Topolino* based on Hemingway's stories. "We had these artists read *Forty-Nine Stories* and left them free to choose a

Additional information in this section was provided by Plume Beuchat.

Topolino's Davide Catenacci. Courtesy Davide Catenacci.

story to adapt," Cavazzano remembers. "They had complete freedom, both in the characters and drawing style. It fills me with pride to have had such extraordinary creators involved in this project. It's unique and still relevant."

The comics aren't straight adaptations, per se. Guido Scala's *Old Man and the Sea* riff includes bits of Steven Spielberg's *Jaws* and even a ghost story. They are more mash-ups of Hemingway's story elements, grand silliness, and Disney's comic book sensibilities. In *Topolino* #2341, a six-page article explained the project, praised Hemingway's writing, and proclaimed, "The real life of Hemingway was extraordinary, rich with great travel and marvelous adventure. And it was just this characteristic that convinced our artists to search for a point of contact between Ernest and Walt [Disney]."

Given that both Walt Disney and Hemingway were volunteer ambulance drivers for the Red Cross in World War I, it seems strange that no one has written a story in which they cross paths. As one of my colleagues pointed out, the young Hemingway was in Paris before being sent to Italy, so the idea that he and Disney could have crossed paths is not entirely ludicrous. The opportunity remains.

"His work is fuel for imagination," says Catenacci, now managing editor of comics in the publishing department of Disney Licensed Products. "Hemingway's writings are an inexhaustible source of inspiration for dreamers who transform their dreams in stories." He adds a personal note: "As a journalist and a writer, I appreciate his marvelous style. As a reader, I have always felt richer at the end of his books. "The Short Happy Life of Francis Macomber" makes me shiver even now, as I write the title."

For the 8 X 8 . . . 49 series, each story was accompanied with a background essay by writer Fausto Vitaliano, who was hired by Ezio Sisto, *Topolino*'s managing editor. Before the project was announced, Sisto invited Vitaliano to lunch and asked him what he thought of the restaurant. "I replied that it seemed like a clean and well-lighted place," remembers Vitaliano. "He asked me if I liked Hemingway. I replied: 'Who doesn't?'"

#1642 (1987)

Uncle Scrooge and the Old Man and the Sea

The residents of a small island are desperate to find new ways to attract tourists and make money, so the community organizes a fishing competition. Chaos ensues when a giant shark disrupts the competition and destroys the pier. To the distress of the businessmen on the island, the terrified tourists immediately leave. Zio Paparone (Uncle Scrooge McDuck)—who boasts of having fought the great shark—is summoned to save the day. Adventure follows, and the shark turns out to be not only friendly but also toothless. The shark becomes the island's main tourist attraction and mascot, as he flaunts a brand-new set of teeth made by a local dentist.

#2278 (1999)

In Hemingway's centennial year, Papa shows up to inspire adventure and courage in Mickey Mouse.

In *Per Chi Suona il Campanello?* Mickey comes back to his hometown after a long trip, but instead of being welcomed, he is scolded by Minnie. Distraught, he goes home, turns down an expedition into the Amazon, and determinedly sets out to find a real job. Just as Mickey is about to leave, however, Hemingway knocks on his door and interviews him for a story about his adventures.

Mickey delves into ridiculous descriptions of pseudo-adventures, mostly implausible, of his exploits in the Sahara, in the jungle, at sea, et cetera. He tells of how he once hijacked a fishing boat and reeled in large plastic fish full of floppy disks of stolen information. An enthusiastic Ernest, who tells a few tales of his own, encourages Mickey's tall tales.

Ernest's admiration lifts Mickey's spirits, and he decides to go to the Amazon after all. Ernest promises to publish his adventures and inspire others to follow in his footsteps. As Mickey leaves, Hemingway says to himself, "I

Hemingway in *Topolino*, 1999.

saved one of the last adventurous hearts from giving up on his own passion. Does that not seem like much?" He vanishes as he walks away.

Written by Alessandro Sisti, the story features art by Graziano Barbaro, who used Yousuf Karsh's famous portrait as the basis for his depiction of Hemingway.

#2341 (2000)

In *Il papero che volle farsi re* (The Duck Who Wanted to Make Himself King), Marco Forcelloni loosely adapted "The Capital of the World," exchanging Hemingway's waiter with bullfighting aspirations for Donald Duck, who overcomes a steampunk robot in the Middle Ages.

#2369 (2001)

Writer/artist Nicola Tosolini's story *Sahara,* starring Mickey and Minnie Mouse, tips its hat to Hemingway's "The Short Happy Life of Francis Macomber" with this desert tale, which puts Mickey and Minnie Mouse at the center of mystery about the lost pyramid of King Tut.

#2345 (2000)

Cowboy Blues by Stefano Turconi is based on "The Undefeated." In Mouse Groove, Texas, Goofy is a despondent blues musician. He is kicked out of every bar in town, because the proprietors only want country music. His producer, however, gives him a videotape to learn how to play and look like a cowboy. All the cringe-worthy cowboy stereotypes are on display, but Goofy puts his heart and soul into the effort. His first gig is at a rodeo, which goes about as well as can be expected when Goofy ends up in the bull-riding competition. But in the end, even the bull joins Goofy's band to sing the Cowboy Blues, his combination of blues and country music.

Turconi, who adapted the story, calls it one of his favorite tales, although he did not choose it for "ease of adaptation." "All the stories are, from a Disney point of view, very complicated, given the vast amount of topics that cannot be addressed in Disney comics—from death, to hunting, to bullfighting. "In fact, I moved the setting from the Spanish bullfights to an American rodeo," Turconi says.

#2349 (2000)

Alessandro Perina's *Bad Boys* is based on "The Killers." Two gangster-looking characters stomp into a diner carrying suspicious-looking violin cases. Things degenerate as they raid the kitchen, tie up the cook (Mickey) and the waiter (Goofy), and interrogate them about a character named Plotty, a frequent customer. After the gangsters wait for Plotty for hours, they send Mickey out to find him and bring him to the diner, which he does. A heated conversation leads to the menacing men teaching Plotty a "musical lesson" right there in the diner. They pull out musical instruments instead of weapons—and break out in song. Plotty can't resist joining in on the piano. The Bad Boys—as their band is called—are reunited. People flock to listen to them play that night, right in the diner.

#2353 (2001)

Zio Paperone e l'equivoco scottante (Uncle Scrooge and the Big Misunderstanding), by Andrea Freccero, is based on "A Day's Wait."

#2357 (2001)

Un giorno perfetto (A Perfect Day), by Marco Palazzi, is based on "Big Two-Hearted River." Palazzi remembers the 8 X 8 . . . 49 project fondly and recalls when he and his Accademia Disney colleagues adapted some of Hemingway's stories, "trying to keep their original spirit and atmosphere alive by using Disney's standard characters."

"The main challenge was how to adapt Hemingway's realism to the Disney world and, in some cases, the rawness inside the stories," Palazzi says.

Palazzi's singular problem was adapting Hemingway's iconic, two-part short story "Big Two-Hearted River" into a nearly wordless, eight-page comic: "In my case, the river location was perfect to describe the sense of introspection—using no dialog balloons at all. There's a sense of melancholy, not very common in Disney, that came out in the finale."

Palazzi adds a Philip K. Dick–like twist to the story, when the perfect fishing day is revealed to be an artificial experience. Mickey exits nature through an elevator in a tree trunk and returns all his fish—robots!—to a park employee, who resets them with a screwdriver for future fishermen.

"It was a beautiful experience for me and a great honor to have the opportunity to translate Hemingway's words in the figurative language of comics," Palazzi says.

#2361 (2001)

Mickey e i due cuochi (Mickey and the Two Cooks), by Giuseppe Zironi, is based on "The Battler" (or, as it's called in Italy, *"Il Lottatore"*).

Zironi was drawn to the story because it features a seemingly ordinary person "who randomly finds himself in a particularly weird and dangerous situation . . . just like Cary Grant in *North by Northwest,*" he says.

Zironi's changed a few details: "The main character (Mickey) is a journalist, instead of a fighter, and his companions are two crazy and fairly dangerous cooks. Everything else is identical, including the whole creepy vibe."

When the original 8 X 8 . . . 49 project was wrapping up, all the artists presented their works to the new director of *Topolino,* Claretta Muci. "When my turn came, I spoke a lot about the most disturbing details in the story—there were many—and as I was speaking I could see the smile on her face slowly disappearing," Zironi remembers. "If there was someone crazy in the story, I'm sure that she thought it was me."

Topolino artist Giuseppe Zironi, 2001. Used with permission of Zironi.

Hemingway continues to show up in comics because, Zironi says, "he became a legendary character who adventurously lived through dramatic events of the twentieth century."

Italians in particular feel a kinship with Hemingway because of the author's time in Italy during World War I. Hemingway worked for American Red Cross on the Italian front during World War I, and in his book *A Farewell to Arms,* he "was also one of the first to tell the Italian defeat of Caporetto, an event that deeply marked the history of my country in those years," remembers fellow Disney comic book creator Stefano Turconi. This, combined with the fact that his books benefited from an excellent Italian translation (many are done by Fernanda Pivano, one of the best translators of the time) and excellent publishers (Hemingway was a friend of Giangiacomo Feltrinelli, who first published *Doctor Zhivago* in the West), made Hemingway very popular in Italy.

Author James McGrath Morris (*The Ambulance Drivers: Hemingway, Dos Passos, a Friendship Made and Lost in War* [2017]) and Marino Perissinotto, an Italian historian, further deepened that kinship in 2019 when they found the name of the previously unknown soldier who died standing next to Hemingway during a mortar attack along the Piave River. That soldier, Private Fedele Temperini, took the brunt of the blast and died, unwittingly saving the life of an 18-year-old Hemingway.

"This excites the fantasies of Italians, who love to have been part of such a famous American writer's life," Zironi says.

The adaptations of Hemingway's work in the movies made his writing more accessible in Italy, and Hemingway's relationship with Cuba, a country that Italians feel very connected to, only strengthens that bond,

Zironi says. "When I was a kid in the '60s, . . . I was particularly amazed by *The Snows of Kilimanjaro* with Gregory Peck and Africa—adventurous, melancholic, featuring wild animals—everything I wished for! And everything that I maybe still wish for."

At the same time, however, Hemingway's work itself made a lasting impact in Italy. "It's definitely due to his writing style: dry, with no sugar-coating and always clearly built around specific events. Hemingway defined a style which is very pleasant to adapt to, and that fulfills the need of adventure," Zironi says. "I love characters that end up being involved in situations they didn't call for, which is a recurring situation in Hemingway's stories. Cartoonists themselves are similar to that as well. They stay home all day drawing incredible adventures that they will never actually live, and Hemingway can be a perfect alter ego for them."

All the stories that the artists had created were supposed to be published in one book, although the project was never realized. "Mine was supposed to be in black and white, with halftone gray, like the old stories of the '50s," Zironi says. "Unfortunately the book was never made, and the stories were published in small format and in color only in the *Topolino* magazine."

He still holds out hope that project will be published. "I would be very, very happy. Never say never."

#2365 (2001)

Nelle acque (In the Water), by Manuela Razzi, is based on "After the Storm." When Donald Duck hears about a ship filled with gold that was lost during a storm, he sets out to find it. Once he locates the shipwreck underwater, he can see the treasure through a window—but he's thwarted by a locked door. Getting locked out is a "beffard sconfitta" or "mocking defeat," which is pretty Hemingwayesque.

Fausto Vitaliano on Hemingway

Here Fausto Vitaliano remembers his time with *Topolino,* working on the Hemingway project, during which he wrote all the prose introductions to each story. Trained as journalist, Vitaliano later established himself as a comic book writer and novelist.

Hemingway's prose is quite visual, which makes it close to the world of comics.

This [8 X 8 . . . 49] was the very first work I did for *Topolino* magazine. It gave me also the opportunity to speak for the first time with Giorgio Cavazzano, one of the living legends of comics. I didn't know how to address him.

Illustration of Fausto Vitaliano by Greta Crippa, available at Bēhance, https://www.behance.net/gretacrippa.

The emotion was such that I called him Giorgio, and I regretted that excessive familiarity a second later. The Maestro didn't mind. A few years later, Cavazzano illustrated one of my stories for *Topolino #2626*, *Paperoga maestro di chiassofono meccanico.* . . .

Thanks to the work I did on 8 X 8 . . . 49, I introduced Hemingway's short stories to my eldest son, Nicholas, who greatly appreciated them and even prepared a school project on Hemingway. Hemingway should not only be read but, above all, reread. I envy those who read his work for the first time. I still remember the emotion felt when, at 15, I read "Hills Like White Elephants" for the first time. It's hard for me to describe that feeling. I guessed that the two characters were talking about an abortion, but I had no chance to ask anyone if that was really the subject. I was so struck by the dialogue that it inspired an exchange in my latest novel, *La grammatica della corsa* [The Grammar of the Race]. I hope Hemingway wouldn't be offended.

It is a widely known fact that Hemingway loved Italy and visited many places in my country.

He had been hospitalized in Milan, a period that inspired *A Farewell to Arms*. I live in Milan. I often pass by Via Armorari and read the plaque which reads: "In the summer of 1918, Ernest Hemingway was welcomed and cared for in this building."

The plaque in Milan, Italy, memorializing Hemingway's hospital stay. Photo Courtesy David Bramhall.

NELL'ESTATE DEL 1918
IN QUESTO EDIFICIO
ADIBITO A OSPEDALE DELLA CROCE ROSSA AMERICANA

ERNEST HEMINGWAY

FERITO SUL FRONTE DEL PIAVE
FU ACCOLTO E CURATO

COSÍ NACQUE LA FAVOLA VERA DI
"ADDIO ALLE ARMI"

2001–2005

The Hemingway Comic Universe Expands

Barry Ween Boy Genius 2.0 #2 (2001)

Judd Winick re-creates a famous photo of a bare-chested, aging Hemingway posing in front of a mirror, wearing boxing gloves.

In the caption, Barry Ween's journal paraphrases Hemingway—"In *The Sun Also Rises,* Ernest Hemingway describes genius as the ability to learn at a greater velocity"—but mixes up the attribution.

The actual quotation comes from *Death in the Afternoon:* "A great enough writer seems to be born with knowledge. But he really is not; he has only been born with the ability to learn in a quicker ratio to the passage

Hemingway in *The Adventures of Barry Ween Boy Genius* 2.0. © Oni Press, Inc.

of time than other men and without conscious application, and with an intelligence to accept or reject what is already presented as knowledge."

Yet, Ween's observations cut pretty close to the bone: "For a suicidal drunk with a pathological fear of latent homosexuality, Papa did all right."

Frazz (Sunday, April 15, 2001)

Jef Mallett's *Frazz* daily comic strip has been packed with Hemingway jokes and references through the years (see the *Frazz* strip in the section on Karsh, p. 2). The strip revolves around Edwin "Frazz" Frazier, an elementary school janitor, triathlete, and all-around Renaissance man. Many of the strips are about Caulfield, an eight-year-old who loves to dress up like his literary heroes—including Hemingway.

"I think comics are a reliable mirror to the culture in general, or at least the part of it that reads, and Hemingway is a huge and relatable presence in that culture," says Mallett.

A longtime endurance runner, Mallett returns to Hemingway for inspiration. "And when I have a particularly big event coming up, I'll reread or listen to *The Old Man and the Sea*," he says. "It gives me a lot of strength, and it never gets old. (Hey, clichés become clichés for good reason sometimes.)"

He continues: "This was a man who lived life fully, absorbed it and wrote about it. That's how I try to approach writing. I fall a bit short of Hemingway, but who doesn't?"

Hemingway reference in *Frazz.*
Frazz © 2001 Jef Mallett. Dist. By
ANDREWS MCMEEL SYNDICA-
TION. Reprinted with permission.
All rights reserved.

Blanche Goes to Paris #1 (2001)

A self-professed "big Hemingway fan," Rick Geary included the author in two panels of *Blanche Goes to Paris*. "I felt it only natural to include him in a story that takes place in Paris in 1921," Geary says. Hemingway's *The Old Man and the Sea* is the first work of "serious" literature that he had ever read, at age 13.

"Later on I read his other novels and came to appreciate what a revolutionary influence he was on American writing," Geary says. "But the simple power of *The Old Man* has stayed with me over the years, and the Hemingway 'style' overall has given me lessons in the art of unadorned storytelling."

Dark Horse later reprinted *Blanche Goes to Paris,* in the *Adventures of Blanche* hardcover collection (2009). Geary also illustrated Hemingway in one panel of Steve Vance's *Big Book of Vice* (1998).

Above: Blanche Goes to Paris cover, 2001.

Following pages: Hemingway in *Blanche Goes to Paris* #1, 2001. © Rick Geary. Reprinted with permission. All rights reserved.

M. Satie and M. Picasso have twice taken me to the home of their American friends, Miss Stein and Miss Toklas, two eccentric ladies who live together as if married.

Miss Stein, a writer of note herself, has penned the rather minimal libretto for our opera-ballet.

She glories in the role of counsellor and patroness to the young artists of all nations who have gravitated to Paris since the Great War.

Their salon is a lively and stimulating gathering-place, where no idea is too radical or outrageous for discussion.

One evening last week, M. Picasso and a boistrous American journalist named Hemingway escorted me on a tour of the most notorious cafes and night-clubs of the Montmartre district.

As you know, I am no lover of "night-life," but I went along, for the sake of being a "good fellow."

I sipped absinthe...

and witnessed the most brazen sort of dancing.

At one establishment I was enthralled by an ensemble of American Negroes, who played a new form of popular music called "JAZZ."

They worked without a score—from their own intuition! Can this be the future of music?

I must say that M. Picasso, despite his reputation, has acted the perfect gentleman.

Not so Mr. Hemingway—too easily the victim of drink.

Beware the Creeper #1, 2, 5 (2003)

In writer Jason Hall's *Beware the Creeper,* 1920s Paris is the stage, and Hemingway is one of the bit players in a violent melodrama. The main story focuses on twin sisters Judith and Madeline Benoir, a Surrealist painter and a playwright. After Judith is raped by an aristocrat, a mysterious figure (the Creeper) exacts revenge on the man's family.

Appearing in three issues, Hemingway throws punches and ponders the Lost Generation.

"To be sure, we went pretty broad with our portrayal of Hemingway, but it was intended as an affectionate caricature," says artist Cliff Chiang. "He provided a nice contrast with the more abstract pretensions of the Surrealists, while his legendary lust for life made for some humorous cameos."

He adds, "It's his final appearance in the book that is the most important, when he gives some sincere, hard-earned advice to our lovelorn heroine."

That advice centers on the American bohemian set coming to Paris to find—and reinvent—themselves.

"Well, we drink to escape," Hemingway says in *Beware the Creeper.* "We could always drink ourselves to death, but then suicide is the coward's way out. Maybe you could just become someone else . . . less painful, anyway."

Hemingway in *Beware the Creeper,* 2003. © DC Comics.

Fishermen Story, 2004. © Caravelle.

Fisherman Story: En Attendant Hemingway (2004)

In Irek Konior's French graphic novel about monster-sized fish and a small fishing village, Hemingway is the equivalent of Godot from Samuel Beckett's *Waiting for Godot.* The difference? Hemingway actually shows up to save the day.

The Left Bank Gang (2005), *Pocket Full of Rain and Other Stories* (2008), and *Pop!* (2016)

Norwegian artist Jason (the pen name of John Arne Sæterøy) is best known for his minimalist, often dialogue-free, panels populated with people or anthropomorphic animals. Hemingway gets both treatments.

In *The Left Bank Gang,* Hemingway—here a graphic novelist—F. Scott Fitzgerald, and company are portrayed as humanoid animals.

"I'm still not sure if [Hemingway is] a cat or a dog, actually!" Jason says. This particular story, he explains, was born out of reading biographies, particularly *Hemingway vs Fitzgerald* by Scott Donaldson and *Hemingway: The Paris Years* by Michael Reynolds. In fact, the French edition of Reynolds's book was originally called, simply, *Hemingway.*

In one sequence, Hemingway comforts a wounded Fitzgerald, whose wife has insulted the size of his manhood.

"It's completely normal," Hemingway assures him in a following panel. "Don't listen to Zelda. She's crazy."

The rest of the book is reimagined history, culminating in a heist inspired by Stanley Kubrick's movie *The Killing*. See Jace Gatzemeyer's further examination of *The Left Bank*, in this volume (pp. 81–91).

Hemingway appears three times in Jason's work, most recently in *Pop!* in a one-page portrait of a suicidal Hemingway.

• • •

In the story collection *Pocket Full of Rain and Other Stories,* Jason places Hemingway directly in one of his own famous short stories. In "The Killers," a pair of hit men hold Nick Adams and some diner employees captive as they wait for their target to show up: a boxer who ran afoul of their unnamed client. After the killers leave, Adams, Hemingway's literary alter ego, goes to warn the boxer, who is holed up in a boardinghouse.

In Jason's story, however, he substitutes Hemingway for the boxer, and the result is a Hemingway stand-in meeting the author himself (a device

One-page portrait of a suicidal Hemingway in *Pop!,* 2016. © Jason. Reprinted with permission. All rights reserved.

This and following page: Anthropomorphized Hemingway and Ftizgerald in *The Left Bank Gang,* 2005. © Jason. Courtesy Fantagraphics Books (www.fantagraphics.com). Reprinted with permission. All rights reserved.

also used in *Nathan Never,* see pp. 35–37, this volume). The panel in which Hemingway says "They've already destroyed my memory" may be a reference to the electroconvulsive therapy Hemingway received at the Mayo Clinic in 1960 and 1961, which disrupted his short-term memory.

The publication dates given here reflect the work's English-language translation release, minus *Pop!* which has not yet been released in the United States.

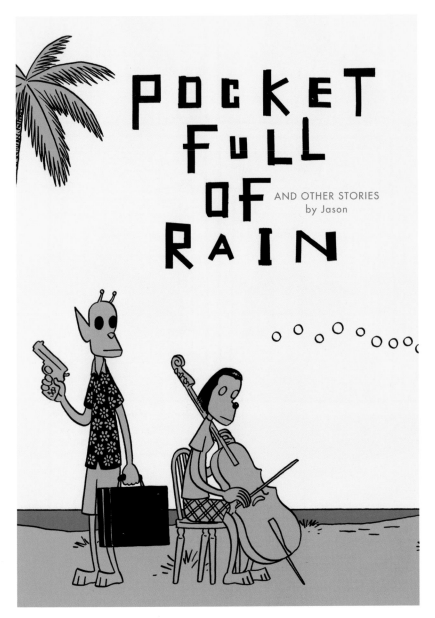

Left: Cover of *Pocket Full of Rain and Other Stories.*

Following pages: Hemingway in *Pocket Full of Rain and Other Stories,* 2008. © Jason. Courtesy Fantagraphics Books (www.fantagraphics.com). Reprinted with permission. All rights reserved.

THE LAST FEW YEARS OF HIS LIFE HEMINGWAY SUFFERED FROM PARANOIA. HE WAS CONVINCED THAT HE WAS BEING WATCHED, AND THAT AGENTS WERE GOING TO ARREST HIM AND LOCK HIM UP IN JAIL.

A PROGRAM OF ELECTROSHOCK THERAPY HAD NO POSITIVE EFFECT.

ERNEST HEMINGWAY COMMITTED SUICIDE IN 1961.

SOURCE:
"PAPA HEMINGWAY"
A.E. HOTCHNER

"I Think We Should Steal Some Money"

The Left Bank Gang and Jason's Hemingway

Jace Gatzemeyer

In the summer of 1924, Ernest Hemingway wrote to Ezra Pound about what he called "the ruin of my finances and literary career." "Now we havent got any money anymore I am going to have to quit writing and I never will have a book published," he complained, "I feel cheerful as hell."[1] Unemployed and making no money from his writing, Hemingway may well have considered more risky methods for coming into cash quickly.

In his 2005 graphic novel *The Left Bank Gang,* originally published in French as *Hemingway,* critically acclaimed Norwegian cartoonist Jason (John Arne Sæterøy) imagines what might have happened if Hemingway *had* acted on these sorts of thoughts. While the first half of Jason's book, his eighth graphic novel, constitutes a thoughtful and precise graphic representation of Hemingway in 1920s Paris, the second half happens to be a crime thriller inspired by Stanley Kubrick's 1956 film noir *The Killing.*

In Jason's characteristic minimalist method, *The Left Bank Gang* depicts characters as anthropomorphic animals drawn in a clean *ligne claire* style.[2] Yet in spite of its fantastical plot and simple style, Jason's genre-bending representation of Hemingway and the Paris expatriate scene of the 1920s is rich, thoughtful, and, when it wants to be, meticulously accurate.

In the first half of the book, apart from the fact that in this fictional world Hemingway and his friends—including F. Scott Fitzgerald, James Joyce, and Ezra Pound—are struggling cartoonists rather than writers, Jason stays faithful to the real atmosphere of 1920s Paris as Hemingway experienced it. On the opening page, for instance, Hemingway meets Pound on the streets of the Latin Quarter. "I just got back from Rapallo," says Pound. "Say, I'm on my way to the Closerie. Care to join me?" "I'd be delighted," Hemingway replies, "but Gertrude Stein is having me for dinner. Maybe I'll see you later at the Dingo?"[3]

Other scenes include just as much true-to-life detail. In one, Hemingway sits quietly as Stein lectures him on the finer points of cartooning:

The Left Bank Gang, 2005. © Jason. Courtesy Fantagraphics Books (www.fantagraphics.com). Reprinted with permission. All rights reserved.

"Avoid narrative captions. Never ever write 'a little later.' It's unnecessary. The reader can figure it out." In another, Fitzgerald gets too drunk, again, and stands on his chair, singing, "Yes, we have no bananas, we have no bananas today." At one point, he visits Shakespeare and Company to pick up his mail and finds a rejection letter from the *Century* magazine.[4] Jason admits that *The Left Bank* is "pretty much based on" Hemingway's *A Moveable Feast,* which he considers "a terrific book." "Who knows how much of it is true," he says, "but it's got some great writing in it."[5]

A Moveable Feast, of course, is Hemingway's posthumously published memoir of his time in Paris during the 1920s. Chicago journalist Sherwood Anderson gave Hemingway a letter of introduction to art collector and salon hostess Gertrude Stein, who welcomed Hemingway into her social circle of artists and provided some early mentorship. Stein and her partner, Alice B. Toklas, would become godmothers to Hemingway's first son, John "Bumby." In Paris, he would also become friends with F. Scott Fitzgerald, who had just published *The Great Gatsby* and would connect Hemingway with Maxwell Perkins, who would become his editor at Scribner's.

Indeed, some events in *The Left Bank Gang* are adapted almost directly from *A Moveable Feast.* For instance, early in the book Hemingway sits down at the Café du Dôme to work on his comics, but when he sees a woman sitting across from him, he decides to draw her instead. With this page, Jason re-creates visually a particularly memorable passage from Hemingway's memoir: "A girl came in the cafe; and sat by herself at a table near the window. She was very pretty with a face fresh as a newly minted coin if they minted coins in smooth flesh."[6]

Jason even includes the dubious "matter of measurements" story, in which Fitzgerald reveals his insecurity about the size of his penis. Sitting together at a bar, Fitzgerald tells Hemingway, "Zelda keeps on saying that I could never satisfy a woman because . . . it's too little." "Let's go check," Hemingway responds. After a quick trip to the bathroom, he reassures Fitzgerald, "It's completely normal. Don't listen to Zelda. She's crazy"; to prove it, he takes Fitzgerald to the Louvre to look at the nudes: "Did you see that one? See? And that one, look."[7]

"It probably never happened," says Jason, "but it's such a great story that I had to include it in the comic."[8]

But halfway through *The Left Bank Gang,* things take a turn toward the fantastical. While in the park with his son, Hemingway witnesses a thief stealing a woman's purse, and in the next scene, over drinks with Fitzgerald, Joyce, and Pound, he suddenly declares, "I think we should steal some money."[9] Together they conspire to rob the cash office at a horse-racing track, and the latter half of the book depicts the attempted robbery from the perspective of each character.

As might be expected, things go horribly wrong. Zelda and her lover, the French aviator Edouard Jozan, betray the Left Bank Gang and take the

Hemingway and Fitzgerald
in *The Left Bank Gang*.

money. However, in another twist, Zelda betrays Jozan, intending to keep the money for herself and Pound, with whom she has been having a second affair. Zelda shoots Jozan, who shoots her in return, and then she also shoots the oblivious Joyce, who stumbles on the scene accidentally. In the end, Zelda, Jozan, and Joyce die; the money burns up in Zelda's apartment; and Hemingway, Fitzgerald, and Pound end up with nothing but confusion.

Of this sensational second half of the book, Jason recalls, "I had the concept for a long time, but not the story. Then I watched *The Killing* by Stanley Kubrick one night, really enjoyed it, and wanted to do something in that style—to have one event seen from different perspectives." Not only did the style seem appealing, he says, but also "I couldn't help seeing how my characters fit into the plot of the movie. Hemingway in the Sterling Hayden part, Fitzgerald as Elisha Cook Jr., and Zelda as Marie Windsor. Ezra Pound seemed to fit as the traitor since later, in World War II, he ended up on the side of Mussolini and the Fascists."[10] Pleased at the time with this symmetry, Jason admits to having "some regrets" today about splitting the narrative in this jarring way: "The first half turned out better than expected, I think, and the second half is almost a bit anticlimactic. I wish I had skipped all that and rather have the gang go to Pamplona for further adventures."[11]

Despite his misgivings, Jason has a bit of a reputation for warping genres by juxtaposing the ordinary and the fantastic. His breakout 2001 graphic novel, *Hey Wait . . .* , for instance, tells the tragic story of a childhood friendship cut short by a sudden death, but interjected into the dramatic scenes are strange and inexplicable, almost surrealistic events, such as a pterodactyl snatching a kite or a man walking around on stilts.[12] Likewise, in one of his most highly praised books, *I Killed Adolf Hitler,* Jason takes a sci-fi thriller about a time-traveling hit man and slowly turns it into a classic love story.[13] "It's bringing those worlds together—juxtaposing them—that's interesting," he says. "That's the thing, that meeting between the everyday and the fantastic that I find interesting or at least fun."[14]

But why such an interest in Hemingway? "I find his life interesting," says Jason. "He took a big bite out of life, you might say. I'm pretty much the opposite of that, I don't hunt and have no interest in bullfighting. But I think you can learn something from his attitude to life."[15] Fittingly enough, Jason first encountered the legendary author through the comics: "I discovered Hemingway through [Hugo Pratt's] *Corto Maltese* [see pp. 17–18, this volume]. In one of the stories, taking place in Italy in World War I, there is a character named Hernestway. It's not a realistic portrayal of Hemingway, but I became curious and started reading his books."[16]

Jason not only read most of Hemingway's work ("I prefer the early short stories [and] the first two novels, *The Sun Also Rises* and *A Farewell to Arms*") and most of the biographies ("My favorite Hemingway biography, I would say, is the five volume set by [Michael] Reynolds"), but he also read most of the letters: "I've read three of the letter volumes, and got vol 4 around somewhere, waiting. Will look forward to vol 5." For *The Left Bank Gang,* apart from *A Moveable Feast,* he says, he drew from several of his favorites: "Reynolds's [*Hemingway: The Paris Years*] and [Scott] Donaldson's [*Hemingway vs Fitzgerald: The Rise and Fall of a Literary Friendship*] books were the main inspiration. *Fitzgerald and Hemingway: A Dangerous Friendship* by [Matthew J.] Bruccoli as well."[17]

Though he describes himself as "the opposite" of Hemingway, Jason does believe the author has had an impact on his life's direction. After spending 14 years in Oslo, he felt "a bit fed up": "My life seemed to consist of going to the studio in the morning and going back the same way in the evening, and to stop by the comic-book shop once a week. . . . I was in my mid-30s, but I hadn't really traveled anywhere."[18]

But it was Hemingway, he says, who "inspired . . . my period of travels in my 30s," during which time he lived in Liège and Brussels in Belgium, New York and Seattle in the United States, and even in Paris for five months, before settling in Montpellier, France. In fact, this "period of travels" also recalls for Jason a point of similarity with Hemingway and his fellow expats. "In my mid-30s," he says, there was a time when "I had some doubts about my choice of profession. I could only afford a small one-room apartment, so I could relate to Hemingway, Joyce and other struggling writers at that time also worrying about money."[19]

One scene in *The Left Bank Gang* was inspired by this period of doubt: a conversation between Hemingway, Joyce, and Pound. "Why do we do comics?" asks Pound, and Joyce answers, "It's too late now. It's the only thing I know how to do." Asked if he wants to quit, Hemingway answers, "No, but . . . I'm tired of fretting about the money all the time, not knowing if I'll be able to pay next month's rent."[20] Of this scene, Jason says, "I can't really think of another job where I'd be happy. I don't know what I'd do today if I hadn't read comics as a kid."[21]

Jason also sees some similarities between his own and Hemingway's approach to storytelling. While he has no grand explanation for his simplistic, anthropomorphic-animals style—"They were easier to draw, the animal characters, it was less of a pain in the ass than the realistic style"—he does find some connections between this style and Hemingway's pared-down prose: "Just as with Hemingway, it's a very basic, meat-and-potatoes type language. I try to do the same in my comics, to avoid unnecessary effects and just tell the story as simply as possible."[22]

When things get too "arty," says Jason, "you almost get the feeling of the cartoonist not trusting the story."[23] Jason has turned this approach into a maxim of which Hemingway might approve: "If I have some sort of rule in my comics, it's to not tell everything, to leave some secrets for the reader to discover. Has that something to do with Hem's iceberg theory? Maybe."[24]

Indeed, this notion of omitting details to "leave some secrets" for the reader sounds very much like Hemingway's own theory of omission. Like

Anthropomorphized Hemingway in *The Left Bank Gang*.

This and facing page: Hemingway and Fitzgerald in *The Left Bank Gang,*
2005. © Jason. Courtesy Fantagraphics Books (www.fantagraphics.
com). Reprinted with permission. All rights reserved.

Hemingway, Jason believes that one side effect of his simple style may be increased audience participation: "If the characters show no emotion, the readers are encouraged to invest their own emotions in them."[25]

Likewise, Hemingway often expressed his goal of "mak[ing] the person who is reading believe that the things happened to him too."[26] In a 1934 essay, Hemingway wrote, "All good books are alike in that they are truer than if they had really happened and after you are finished reading one you will feel that all that happened to you and afterwards it all belongs to you."[27]

While Hemingway has not appeared in any of Jason's comics since *The Left Bank Gang,* he had previously appeared once in the cartoonist's work. In a mini titled "Papa"—collected in *Pocket Full of Rain and Other Stories*— he adapts to a comics format Hemingway's short story "The Killers" with a metafictional twist, replacing the man pursued by hit men, Ole Andreson, with Hemingway himself.[28]

"The idea for the story came from reading A. E. Hotchner's book [*Papa Hemingway: A Personal Memoir*]," says Jason. "He talks about Hemingway turning paranoid towards the end, that he would point out men and say they were agents out to get him."[29] Of re-creating a Hemingway story this way, Jason says, with "his simple style, it's almost like stage directions, and can easily be turned into comics panels, even without narration." He adds that he would enjoy working on Hemingway again someday. "I'd like to return to Hemingway as a character," he says. "For him to maybe take that trip to Pamplona. And I have an idea for another story that would take place during WWII."[30]

Notes

1. Hemingway to Ezra Pound, July 19, 1924, *The Letters of Ernest Hemingway:* vol. 2, *1923–1925* (New York: Cambridge Univ. Press, 2013), 134, 135.
2. On Jason's distinctive style, particularly in the context of *The Left Bank Gang,* see Jan Baetens, "Man/Mask/Animal: On Characterization and Storytelling in Jason's *The Left Bank Gang,*" *Rivista di Letterature Moderne e Comparate* 70, no. 3 (2017): 295–306.
3. Jason [John Arne Sæterøy], *The Left Bank Gang* (Seattle, WA: Fantagraphics, 2006), 1.
4. Jason, *Left Bank Gang,* 11, 19, 6. While Century rejected his short story "Cat in the Rain" in the summer of 1924, Hemingway was not in Paris when he got the news.
5. Matthias Wivel, "The Jason Interview," *Comics Journal,* no. 294, ed. Gary Groth (Seattle, WA: Fantagraphics, 2011), 62, 63.
6. Hemingway, *A Moveable Feast: The Restored Edition* (New York: Scribner, 2009), 17.
7. Jason, *Left Bank Gang,* 15, 16.
8. Wivel, "Jason Interview," 63.
9. Jason, *Left Bank Gang,* 22.
10. Wivel, "Jason Interview," 64.
11. Jason, email interview with Jace Gatzemeyer, Jan. 24–30, 2019.
12. Jason, *Hey, Wait . . .* (Seattle, WA: Fantagraphics, 2001).

13. Jason, *I Killed Adolf Hitler* (Seattle, WA: Fantagraphics, 2007).

14. Wivel, "Jason Interview," 35.

15. Jason, interview.

16. Wivel, "Jason Interview," 62.

17. Wivel, "Jason Interview," 62; Jason, interview.

18. Wivel, "Jason Interview," 54.

19. Jason, interview.

20. Jason, *Left Bank Gang,* 17–18.

21. Wivel, "Jason Interview," 32.

22. Wivel, "Jason Interview," 61.

23. Wivel, "Jason Interview," 42.

24. Jason, interview.

25. Wivel, "Jason Interview," 43. For more on this, see Scott McCloud's *Understanding Comics: The Invisible Art* (New York: HarperCollins, 1993), 24–59. McCloud argues that the simpler one draws human faces, the more the audience can "see themselves" in it: "Thus, when you look at a photo or realistic drawing of a face you see it as the face of another. But when you enter the world of the cartoon you see yourself" (36).

26. Hemingway, *Moveable Feast,* 181.

27. Hemingway, "An Old Newsman Writes: A Letter from Cuba," in *By-Line: Ernest Hemingway,* ed. William White (New York: Scribners, 1967), 155.

28. Jason, *Pocket Full of Rain and Other Stories* (Seattle, WA: Fantagraphics, 2008), 92–98.

29. Jason, interview; A. E. Hotchner, *Papa Hemingway: A Personal Memoir* (New York: Random House, 1966).

30. Jason, interview.

2006–2013

Hemingway: Illustrated by His Grandson, as Papa the Indie Icon, and His Graphic Canon

Hemingway and Bailey's Bartending Guide to Great American Writers (2006)

Our next entry tips over into the territory of caricature, as painted by Ernest's youngest grandson, Edward Hemingway. Edward is best known for his popular children's books, including the *Bad Apple* and *Tough Cookie*. In 2006, he illustrated *Hemingway and Bailey's Bartending Guide to Great American Writers,* which included illustrated portraits of 43 writ-

Ernest Hemingway with his son Gregory. Sun Valley, Idaho. October 1941. Photo by Robert Capa © Magnum Photos/ International Center of Photography.

ers, such as Dorothy Parker, James Baldwin—and Ernest Hemingway. To date, it marks the only time Edward has painted his grandfather.

"I chose to illustrate him in arguably his most famous period; middle-aged and bearded," Edward remembers. "This is how I approached all of the writers in the book, illustrating them at their most iconic." Likeness is key, Edward says, but "so is some sense of character and personality (and always essential to caricature—humor). The danger is in not finding this overall balance."

Edward was born after his grandfather's death, and he only knew the man through photographs and his writing. "He wasn't discussed much in my family growing up. I don't know why," Edward says. "I guess because both my parents were very private people."

He continues: "I suppose the only image of him that impacted me growing up was the photo of him lying on what looks like a bridge in Idaho with my father and some guns [see p. 92, this volume]. I like it because they both look very happy after what I assume was an adventurous day of hunting. Real father and son stuff."

He's been surprised by his grandfather's frequent appearances in comics. "Historically, . . . comics have been underestimated as a medium, so I was delighted when I saw him included," Edward says.

Hemingway illustration by his grandson Edward.

Harlan Ellison's Dream Corridor #2 (2007)

Harlan Ellison pits himself in a poker game against Hemingway, Dorothy Parker, Mark Twain, and a few others in this bumper splash page between two of the stories of this anthology. Artist Eric Shanower illustrates individualized cards for each of the players, and Hemingway holds cards featuring a bullfight, a safari, and snow on the top of Mount Kilimanjaro.

Shanower used Yousuf Karsh's famous Hemingway portrait for reference in this collection that took a decade to finish.

"Harlan said he'd write the pages if I flew to L.A. and watched over him like a guardian angel. So I did," remembers former Dark Horse editor Diana Schutz. "The pages got written. The book got published. The artwork got returned. I remember nothing about Hemingway."

Hemingway plays poker in *Harlan Ellison's Dream Corridor* #2, March 2007. © Harlan Ellison.

Simpsons Comics #135 (2007)

"The Bald Man and the Sea," *Simpsons Comics* #135, 2007. © Bongo Comics.

OK, Hemingway doesn't actually appear in this *Simpsons* homage, "The Bald Man and the Sea." Here, Homer is a stand-in for Santiago, the "old man" locked in a struggle against himself, the elements and a strong-willed marlin. It goes as well as you might expect.

"When you are dealing with a property that has told hundreds of stories, you have to dig deep," says writer James Bates. "My father-in-law was a big fishing enthusiast, so it was always in the back of my mind to do a fishing story. The Simpsons have a bay, and so I decided to figure out what I could create."

Bates considers straight parodies to be lazy. But a good homage is a different thing: "I love the man against himself wrapped inside man against nature stories. So when the goofy pun 'Bald Man and the Sea' popped into my balding head, the story was born."

There's even an alternate ending.

"My original ending had Homer waking like Santiago, but he noticed his foil (Ned Flanders) getting accolades on TV. Ned had caught the fish after Homer tired it out," says Bates. "Not quite the quiet dignity of Hemingway but very much Homer. D'oh!"

Jesus Christ: In the Name of the Gun (2008)

Eric Peterson's hyper-violent satire casts Hemingway in the buddy-cop genre, in which a vengeful, sandal-wearing Jesus of Nazareth is his partner. Here, the ninjalike Hemingway travels through time, assassinating history's biggest mass murderers with the Son of God.

Begun as a web comic, the series embraces a strong moral core and punk-rock ethos, as well as Hunter S. Thompson's gonzo zaniness.

"I've got more photos of Hemingway and Thompson hanging in my house than I do of my parents," says Peterson, who admits that Hemingway's depiction might be "borderline disrespectful for the writer that I love so much."

Peterson says that in the third book of the series, he "really wanted to home in on the fact that Ernest is a man chased by and chasing the idea of his own strength."

He adds: "The author holds a very special place in my heart. I get a bit miffed that maybe the 'legend' of Hemingway holds a place in the mainstream consciousness more than the work itself. But, I think that's just a part of his legacy. Same goes for Thompson."

The artist Gabo, aka Gabriel Bautista, illustrated Hemingway not only in *The Life After* (see the excerpt on pp. 172–177, this volume) but also in a later chapter of *Jesus Christ: In the Name of the Gun.*

Page 24 from the first series of *Jesus Christ: In the Name of the Gun* in which the son of God meets Hemingway.

Page 25 from the first series of *Jesus Christ: In the Name of the Gun* in which the son of God meets Hemingway.

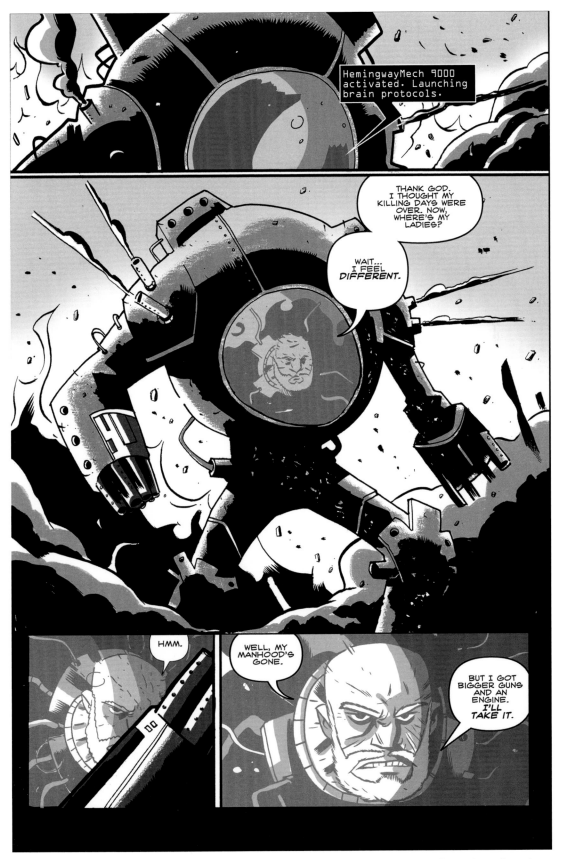

Later in the series of *Jesus Christ: In the Name of the Gun,* Hemingway is reanimated as a cyborg. This page, illustrated by Ryan Cody, appears in *Volume 2, Temporal Death Punch.*

Later in the series of *Jesus Christ: In the Name of the Gun,* Hemingway is reanimated as a cyborg. This page, illustrated by Ryan Cody, appears in *Volume 2, Temporal Death Punch.*

Gabo took over the *Jesus Christ: In the Name of the Gun* artistic duties in Volume 3, *The End of the World*, as seen in this page.

Gabo took over the *Jesus Christ: In the Name of the Gun* artistic duties in *Volume 3, The End of the World,* as seen in this page.

"When I jumped onto the *Name of the Gun* project, Ernest had already gone through a pretty rough and incredible physical transformation in the previous volume," Gabo remembers. "His body had been salvaged and put inside a giant robot, with a glass dome for him to look through. In that instance, all I really had to worry about was capturing his face while doing my best to make it look slightly damaged."

He continues: "In *The Life After* I got to draw Hemingway as an older man, which was a lot easier, as photos of him at an older age were much more readily available for me to use as a reference."

Hemingway Comix (2008)

At one point in his life, benjamin sTone couldn't get enough Hemingway.

"I devoured everything I could in junior high, although I enjoyed reading about war and picnics more than bullfights. My grandmother assured me it was 'a phase' that every man who reads goes through," sTone remembers.

"While not entirely without merit, she chased her comment with a crack about no matter how much 'pain' he was in, 'He took the coward's way out.' As a kid already struggling with mental health issues, it oddly made me read more deeply into it," he says.

In college, sTone majored in English "and took a solid 300-level course about his work, which helped me decide which bits of his works to take and which to leave. *The Sun Also Rises* was beautifully written, yet stirred me little, whereas I've probably read *A Moveable Feast* four times, at least. I liked *For Whom the Bell Tolls* but took a pass on *The Old Man and the Sea*."

"I'm an emotion-based person, and never identified as particularly masculine—these days I get to use the word genderqueer—and looking back, that definitely colored which of his works I still recall fondly and will occasionally reread," sTone says.

He explains: "There was Hemingway without his pants—drunkenly raving about bullfights, reveling in assholes like Jake, seeing nobility where

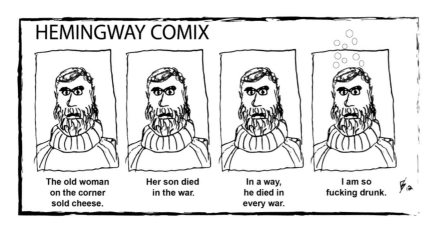

Lovecraft Comix by benjamin sTone

The foul beast awoke from eternal sleep and opened its gaping maw wide, the stench of countless aeons spewing forth.

"No!" screamed Smith, but the tongue of the beast shot forth like a horrid tentacle and encircled his chest, slowly exerting bone-breaking pressure.

My god I'm afraid of vaginas.

Ellison Comix   by benjamin sTone

And those snot-nosed little internet eunuchs, with their torrents and file-sharing, commiting the online equivalent of mugging me...

...they expect me to just stand by and watch as they ...as...what's going on up there? Is that supposed to be me up there? Both of them?

You can bet your ass that somebody's gonna get sued over this one. Is that you, Cameron? Screw you and your blue alien CGI bullshit.

Bradbury Comix   by benjamin sTone

This was many years ago, when my friends and I spent our summers like golden coins that would never lose luster.

Even then, in our carefree days, the future loomed ever before us, a vulture with clock-hand talons.

Yet we all ran on, dodging worry, leaping over fear, and running through sun-lit fields like mortal wind!

I ate nostalgia and shat metaphors.

I saw tedium. And Hemingway *with* his pants, still drunk but hanging out with his friends, or delving into the motivations and the drive of somebody fighting for the right side in another country's civil war.

"He was a macho motherfucker who was somehow startlingly in touch with his emotions. I just sobbed for ages when I finished *A Farewell to Arms,* and wondered how somebody who could write about sadness so beautifully would want to go out and do something like shoot a goddamn elephant. I have a bit of a complex response to him."

The complexity is apparent in sTone's meta *Literary Comix* series, as a parody/meditation on the writer's life. He began posting the series online in 2008, leading off with Hemingway.

"They are mainly just an excuse to ape style for a few panels before dropping a simple punchline," sTone says.

Fort Dudak's Six Pack #3 (2009, also known as *Fort Dudak's Six Panels*)

Fort Dudak's handmade, underground comic featured a meditation on Hemingway's writing advice. In 2009, he became disenchanted with dreaming about being productive at making "comix" (his preferred term for indie, underground-inspired comics) and decided that his obsession with perfect image quality was holding him back, slowing him down, and making him overly critical of his own work.

So, for 30 days straight, he drew improvised, six-panel comix on printer paper. He worked on a clipboard and drew the comix all over Seattle, in parks, coffee shops, et cetera—a productive set of constraints.

Hemingway's influence shows up in the third issue, titled "Scrutiny." "I first recall reading his advice in ninth grade English class. Simply, his advice was to . . . write every day, starting and ending at the same time," Dudak remembers. "And never end a day's session with a completed thought, always stop in the middle so that you have a thread to take up immediately at the start of the next day."

In the panel, Dudak ponders Hemingway's advice on writing—"If that would have kept me productive, lamenting that I am no longer so," he says.

The subtext of the issue, Dudak says, is that self-examination runs the risk of uncovering thoughts of wanting to die. "Basically, it's a joke at his and my expense: Don't commit suicide. The pains of life are better than nonexistence," Dudak says. "Hemingway is representative of all of this and more: productivity vs. deep problems with vice, self-examination and a critical eye vs. self-destruction, depression and suicide."

All through October & November I made a new comic each day. I impressed myself!

Then something happened and I lost the drive.

I don't know what that was.

Maybe it's related to my use of comics to help me quit smoking cigarettes daily (I succeeded btw).

Perhaps I invested too much hope that FINALLY BEING PRODUCTIVE would save my life.*

Mebs I should have made comics at the same time everyday ...

...followed HEMINGWAY'S ADVICE:

* typical artistic hyperbole

① WORK EVERYDAY, AT THE SAME TIME OF DAY, FOR THE SAME AMOUNT OF TIME.

② NEVER FINISH A THOUGHT - -IN THE SAME SESSION.

③ DON'T SHOW YOUR AUDIENCE- -EVERY -THING.

④ DON'T SWALLOW A SHOT GUN; A PROLAPSED INTESTINE AIN'T THAT BAD!!

I'm trying to decide NOW when or if I'm moving back to my home town.

NEXT MONTH?

END OF THE SUMMER?

At least if I continue making comics ...

-then I could handle the seeming backward slide.*

I really want to be near my parents in their last years ...

while they are still healthy ...

but Albany??

Jesus!

The Governor Nelson A Rockefeller Empire State Plaza

If I go, will I make something **more** of it...

or of myself ...

than in the past?

EXIT

* I'm conscious of how it might look if I decide to go home again.

Hemingway in *Fort Dudak's Six Pack #3*.
Courtesy and © Fort Dudak / A.M. Press Comix.

The Old Man and the Sea (2011)

A graphic novel adaptation by illustrator Sono Sanae, this story was issued as a pocket-sized, stand-alone paperback by Manga Bunko. Sono's most recent graphic novel, *Sekigei* (Red Whale, 2018), continues the maritime theme.

Japanese graphic novel adaptation of *The Old Man and the Sea*.

Ichiro (2012)

In *Ichiro*, Ryan Inzana tips his hat to Hemingway by making him a TV survivalist named Harry Morgan (a reference to *To Have and Have Not*). His TV show? It's named *The Battler*, a reference to Hemingway's 1925 short story of the same name.

In the story, Morgan is the favorite TV star of Ichiro, a Japanese American boy who when he visits his grandfather in Japan suddenly finds himself in the realm of gods.

Inzana is a longtime Hemingway fan and, in fact, has allowed us to share a work in progress about the author that began in 2008. Here are five pages from the project, simply titled "Hemingway," which begins in Italy, as Hemingway works as a volunteer for the American Red Cross. More of Inzana's work can be found at www.ryaninzana.com.

Ichiro cover.

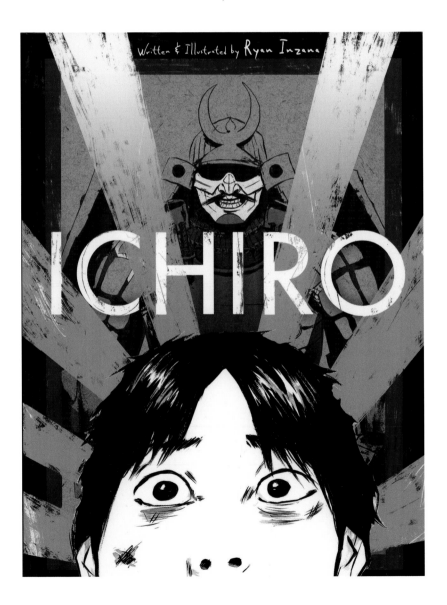

This page from *Ichiro* features Hemingway stand-in Harry Morgan, a reality TV star. Courtesy Ryan Inzana (www.ryaninzana.com).

Ryan Inzana's work in progress, a biographical comic simply titled "Hemingway." Courtesy Ryan Inzana (www.ryaninzana.com).

Ryan Inzana's work in progress, a biographical comic simply titled "Hemingway." Courtesy Ryan Inzana (www.ryaninzana.com).

Ryan Inzana's work in progress, a biographical comic simply titled
"Hemingway." Courtesy Ryan Inzana (www.ryaninzana.com).

Ryan Inzana's work in progress, a biographical comic simply titled "Hemingway." Courtesy Ryan Inzana (www.ryaninzana.com).

Ryan Inzana's work in progress, a biographical comic simply titled "Hemingway." Courtesy Ryan Inzana (www.ryaninzana.com).

"What Did You Write Today, Mister Hemingway?"(2012)

"Recently Discovered! Further Instalments of Famous Six-Word Story" (2019)

Artist Tom Gauld used to provide weekly cartoons inspired by letters published in the *Guardian Review*.

"I think some lost letters or writings by (or maybe about) Hemingway had resurfaced and the letter discussed this," says Gauld. "I think the idea of a 'spiteful letter to my wife' came from the letter."

Hemingway has populated comics since his death, Gauld thinks, because "he seems to be a kind of archetype of the manly, troubled writer. Which is reductive of course, but memorable. If you say Hemingway to most people they will have an idea what he looks like and, even if they haven't read his work, a broad idea of his writing. For my funny cartoons it's easier to use writers that the general public has clear ideas about, like Jane Austen or Agatha Christie."

Gauld adds: "Perhaps the simplicity/clarity of his writing also appeals to cartoonists."

Tom Gauld cartoon.

Hemingway reference in Tom Gauld cartoon.

"Reductive, but memorable" carries a lot of weight, however. "I think it's possibly an inevitable outcome for writers who get famous enough that many people know them but haven't actually read the books," says Gauld. "Maybe this is at its worst when a writer gets reduced to a single word like 'Hemingwayesque' or 'Kafkaesque.' The idea of the writer is getting a life of its own and drifting away from the actual writing."

This became a cultural "feedback loop" in which the writer's name or images becomes a shortcut for the media and cartoonists "use and therefore reinforce," Gauld says. It certainly happened to Gauld when he read *A Farewell to Arms*.

"It turned out to be a lot more thoughtful and romantic than the terse manliness-fest I'd been expecting. So hopefully the simplistic legend of Hemingway at least entices people to read the books, which is better than being forgotten and unread."

Hemingway popped up again in Gauld's work in 2019, this time indirectly. Hemingway never wrote, "For sale: baby shoes, never worn"—but the reference and joke still works.

Historical Society of Oak Park and River Forest prints by Chris Ware (2012)

If you blink, you'll miss him. But the young Hemingway is there, in his hometown of Oak Park, playing football in the street in front of the Frank Lloyd Wright–designed Arthur B. Heurtley House (1902). Ware, best known for his *New Yorker* covers and books such as *Building Stories* (2012) and *Rusty Brown* (2019), also lives in Hemingway's hometown of Oak Park, Illinois. Ware designed this print and two others for the Oak Park River Forest Museum, as part of a fundraiser.

"I included Hemingway because he's, needless to say, an important figure in the town's history, and, well—how couldn't I?" says Ware. "I read *For Whom the Bell Tolls* and *The Sun Also Rises* in high school and it was the first time I realized that writing could be writing and not just storytelling; I was struck even then at how Hemingway carefully tuned the order of sense perceptions and experiences directly to how one would experience them. If that makes any sense. In other words, it felt real."

Inspired by Richard McGuire's comic strip *Here*—which uses embedded frames as windows into other time periods, Ware's prints also capitalize on his love of architecture and his layered, Easter egg–filled storytelling. In another image for this series (not included here), an unidentified pedestrian is reading *For Whom the Bell Tolls*.

Hemingway plays football in his hometown of Oak Park, Illinois.

Arthur B. Heurtley House (1902).

Probably Frank Lloyd Wright's great early masterpiece, it typifies what became known as the Prairie Style, though in vibrant autumnal tones and stretching tiers of sparkling art glass. Wright here visits the second owners of the house, his sister Jane Porter and her husband on the upper veranda, sometime in the early 1940s.

The Potowatami. Residing in various and disparate midwestern locales from what is now Michigan to Wisconsin to Illinois, the Illinois tribe is perhaps best known for the 1812 Battle of Fort Dearborn, suffering profoundly from the "Removal Period" which followed.

For Whom the Bell Tolls (1940). Here, a passing pedestrian reads a jacketed first edition of Hemingway's work sometime in the late 1960s, when the Heurtley house had been divided into apartments and fallen into neglect.

Bowman Dairy Co. was a Chicago Dairy with facilities in Oak Park, amongst others. It was purchased by Dean Foods in 1966.

Ernest Hemingway goes out for a pass in a game of street football on Forest Avenue, c. 1915, while John W. Farson passes by in his automobile.

Wingfoot Express. The Goodyear dirigible was traveling between Grant Park and the White City Amusement Park when it burst into flames on July 21, 1919. Probably unlikely that it would be so visible here, but maybe this historian has a telescope.

THE HISTORICAL SOCIETY OF

OAK PARK *and* RIVER FOREST

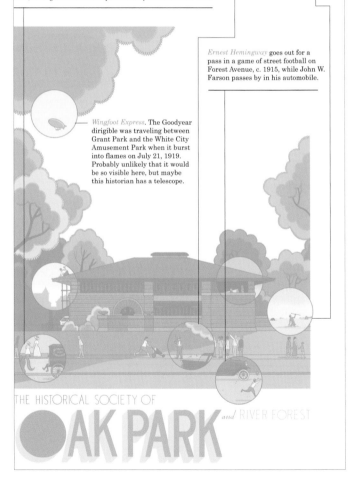

Think of January Jones as the female Indiana Jones—only with a pilot's license.

Jones has a long history among European comics, but here she's teamed up with Hemingway for an adventure. For creator Martin Lodewijk, it was an opportunity to write a story about a family friend who smuggled weapons into Barcelona—and about the Spanish gold that disappeared there.

"I wanted to show some of my misgivings, like George Orwell did, about the Spanish Civil War," Lodewijk says. "Terrible things happened on both sides—which does not mean that I like [Spanish general Francisco] Franco."

When Jones meets Hemingway, they greet one another as old friends and she asks him, "When are you going to write a book about me?"

Joris Ivens, the Dutch documentarian with whom Hemingway was then shooting *The Spanish Earth*, also joins the party. During the happy reunion, a man on the street is kidnapped—and Ivens captures it all on film.

For artist Eric Heuvel, "the challenge was to have Hemingway look the part without his beard. The beret was what made him look the part."

Integrating historical figures and details into the story is a hallmark of the *January Jones* series. Since Heuvel took over as writer in 2015, he has stayed true to the series' history-bending spirit.

Left: Ernest Hemingway (in beret) with film cameraman Joris Ivens and two soldiers during the Spanish Civil War, circa 1937–38. Ernest Hemingway Collection. John F. Kennedy Presidential Library and Museum, Boston.

Following pages: Hemingway in *January Jones.* Courtesy Eric Heuvel / Zaandam.

Wanneer vliegen wij samen over de oceaan, pop?

Ernest!!...Ernest Hemingway!!

Vlieg in mijn armen, Venus!!

En wanneer schrijf jij eens een boek over mij, Pops*)?

*)Hemingway's bijnaam.

Ik schrijf al een tekst voor de film die mijn goede vriend Joris Ivens maakt over de Spaanse tragedie...

Aangenaam!

En dit is mijn mecanicien en co-piloot, Abou B'enkonnu.

Kom mee, we gaan een glas drinken en bijpraten, pop!

Later...

Dus je rekende er 'n beetje op dat ze Rik naar Barcelona wilden ontvoeren...

Maar het vliegveld hier, El Prat, is niet zo groot en we hebben geen Dragon Rapide gevonden!

BARPOPUI R

Ze kunnen natuurlijk ook in Madrid of Cartagena zijn geland. Maar ik heb Rik vaak horen vertellen over zijn oudere broer die met de Internationale Brigades meevecht in Barcelona...En misschien kan die Gerrit Jansen ons verder helpen.

Gerrit Jansen... Maar die ken ik goed!

Ik heb hem nog gefilmd als soldaat van de Hansje Brinker Brigade...Vanwege zijn moed, zijn spierballen en witte bos haar wordt hij hier EL TORO BLANCO genoemd!

Señor! De rekening, por favor!

Dit is de NIEUWE TIJD, compañera! In het revolutionaire Spanje zeggen wij geen 'señor' en al helemaal geen 'por favor'!

Pardon... eh... compañero. Misschien een fooi...

⑬ En 'propinas*)' zijn in de republiek al jaren VERBODEN!! Wij zijn allen gelijk! Compañeras y compañeros!! Geen slaven, geen meesters!! Wij zeggen geen 'buenos dias' maar SALUD! NO PASARAN!!

Mag 'gracias' nog wel?...

*)fooien

Dat is dan precies gepast, compañera, zoals het hoort in het nieuwe Spanje!

Salud, companon... eh...compañero!

Dat is dan afgesproken! Joris brengt jullie in contact met El Toro Blanco...

KUCH!!

?

De straten ten zuiden van de Ramblas vormen een buurt die vroeger El Raval genoemd werd...

...maar ooit door een Franse journalist Barrio Chino werd omgedoopt in Chinese wijk. Er is alleen niets Chinees aan de restaurantjes...

...of aan de winkeltjes, de kroegen en bordelen.

Daar zit 'ie aan zijn stamtafeltje! AHOOOY, GERRIT!!

JORIS! Kom hier met je vrienden... dan drinken we een glas wijn!

Hij is het!!

¡ MANOS ARRIBA!!

AGHK!

Van deze wijn krijg je hoofdpijn, holandés!

¡ DATE PRISA!... OPSCHIETEN! In de auto met 'm!

Ze ontvoeren hem waar we bij zijn!!

JANUARY!! KIJK UIT, POP!!

?!

VRAM

14

Creator Martin Lodewijk on *January Jones*

When I started reading comics, aviation was still something exciting. There were a lot of adventure strips of brave pilots traveling all over the world, setting down in the Kalahari Desert or on a riverbank deep in the Amazon jungle. Most were done in a realistic or semi-realistic style. I think of *Connie, Smilin' Jack, Flyin' Jenny, Steve Canyon, Johnny Hazard* and lots of British series.

I always had a special interest in the female pioneer aviators like Amelia Earhart, Pancho Barnes, Jean Batten, Willa Brown, Amy Johnson—the list goes on. And my friend and artist Eric Heuvel loved drawing flying gear, so we came up with our heroine, January Jones. We decided on a Hergé-like *Tintin* style with dashes of Edgar P. Jacobs [*Blake and Mortimer* creator].

Like Eric, I was always interested in the world between the wars, the twenties and thirties. Not only the planes but also the pulp magazines, Prohibition gangsters, movies and music. Both of us love putting authentic details in our stories. We used little asterisks in the word balloons directing the reader to a small panel underneath the frame saying "authentic"—it's almost a running gag in my comics. So January encounters many historical situations and characters in her stories. Some are "authentic," and some are slightly reworked.

January is one of the many children of US senator Aristides Jones and professor Amaryllis Smith-Jones. Being practical parents, they named their daughters after the month[s] they were born . . . and sons after their state of birth. An elder sister is a famous thriller writer, November Jones, and a younger one, April Jones, is a promising Hollywood actor. You can imagine Eric's and my surprise when the real January Jones [*Mad Men*] became a movie star. She must have been about nine years old when our series started.

Planes in *January Jones*. Courtesy Eric Heuvel / Zaandam.

Martin Lodewijk (*left*) and Eric Heuvel of *January Jones* at a convention in 2016. Photo courtesy Martin Lodewijk.

Our January flies around the world in a red De Havilland Comet DH.88, winning races, setting records, and even winning the Monte Carlo car race across Europe. On the way, she encounters and sometimes teams up with historic scoundrels and spies, detectives and dictators. They include the Queen of Sheba, Nikola Tesla, Albert Einstein, gangster Louis "Lepke" Buchalter, and Butch Cassidy and the Sundance Kid.

Of course, I had read *For Whom the Bell Tolls* and seen the movie, so it isn't strange that Ernest Hemingway pops up in *January Jones*. Together, they encounter Dutch documentary director Joris Ivens, John Dos Passos, Orson Welles, and General Franco.

Kiki de Montparnasse (2012)

In real life, Hemingway wrote the introduction for *Kiki's Memoirs* in 1929, so it's only natural that he show up for a cameo in a graphic novel. Kiki, whose real name was Alice Prin, was a singer, actress, painter, and model, best known as the figure in Man Ray's surrealist photo *Le violon d'Ingres*. She was portrayed here as the Queen of Montparnasse by artist Catel Muller and author Jose-Luis Bocquet.

Kiki de Montparnasse,
May 2012. © Harry N. Abrams.

Twists of Fate (*Los surcos del azar*) (2013)

This World War II story reclaims the lost history of "The Nine" (or La Nueve), a company of Spanish Republicans who enlisted with the Free French Army of Charles de Gaulle after battling Fascist dictator Francisco Franco in Spain.

"When I came across the story of The Nine, I was struck by the epic fact that they were the first to enter occupied Paris," says author and illustrator Paco Roca. "But more than that fact itself, The Nine served me to tell the long journey of people who never stopped fighting against fascism. Their long journey would take them to Hitler's Eagle's Nest. They never surrendered; they said that fighting against fascism was as necessary for them as breathing."

Roca's *Los surcos del azar* was published by Astiberri in Spain, and it went on to be published in France, Italy, Germany, and the Netherlands. In 2018, Fantagraphics published a 320-page English edition titled *Twists of Fate*.

Hemingway enters the story, Roca explains, once The Nine enter Paris. He symbolizes the "tourists" who come to witness the war but are not part of it. In the sequence, the freedom fighters encounter an intoxicated Hemingway, who welcomes them warmly after the liberation of Paris.

But Hemingway wasn't always part of the story, Roca says. During the research phase of the book, Roca reread *For Whom the Bell Tolls,* which takes place during the Spanish Civil War (1936–39). All the pieces started to fall into place when Roca read the memoir of The Nine's captain Raymond Dronne, which mentioned Hemingway as one of those journalists who accompanied the division.

In the graphic novel, Roca uses Hemingway to illustrate how Franco was treated after the war. "Hemingway, who was very involved during the civil war with the Spanish Republic, vowed not to return to Spain until democracy was restored," Roca says. "But, after a few years, he was enjoying the bullfights in Pamplona again. That 'pardon' of the international powers legitimized Franco in power for 40 years."

That said, Hemingway remains one of Roca's favorite authors. Roca had previously referenced Hemingway's work habits, in his quasi-autobiographical strip *Memorias de un hombre en pijamas* (*Memoirs of a Man in Pajamas*) for Spain's *El País* newspaper. In the 2018 animated movie adaptation of the strip, Hemingway actually shows up to offer advice to the protagonist, a comic book author struggling with writer's block.

"Hemingway appears to him and advises him to shoot himself. If he fails, everything will end, but if he survives then he will have something to tell," Roca says.

Hemingway the character continues to appear in comics, literature, and movies because "he is a very powerful character," Roca says. "He has become, due to his suicide, an iconic cliché of the tormented and visceral author."

Above: Hemingway in *Memoirs of a Man in Pajamas.*

Following pages: Hemingway meets The Nine in *Twists Of Fate.* © Paco Roca. Courtesy Fantagraphics Books (www.fantagraphics.com). Reprinted with permission. All rights reserved.

Glory #30 (2012) and Glory #34 (2013)

Glory #30, April 2012. ©
Image Comics, Inc.

Hemingway shoots at a caped villain along Parisian rooftops in a prologue story "*Fantomas: L'Affaire La 'Glory'!*"—illustrated by Roman Muradov, best known for his work in the *New Yorker* and the *New York Times*. It's not the only time Hemingway is a touchstone in Muradov's work (see entry on *kuš!* in this volume, p. 187).

The title character, Glory, is Rob Liefeld's Wonder Woman–esque warrior demoness, which explains why she spans decades. Writer Joe Keatinge took over the character in a later incarnation, adding a backstory with Gertrude Stein, Pablo Picasso, and Hemingway.

"He's my favorite author, so that's where it came from. I wrote this whole history no one is ever going to see, including Glory meeting Hemingway in Spain," says Keatinge. "I just love the way he writes. There's no bullshit. . . . It's all very direct, all very to the point."

In the story, as Glory cradles her prey in a headlock, Hemingway compliments her on the collar. "You flatter me too much, Ernest! I couldn't have captured him alone!" she says. "We may be the lost generation, but we can accomplish great things now that we've found each other."

Sophie Campbell, the arc's chief artist, says Hemingway made an unnamed cameo in the final issue of the series. "I actually didn't want to draw that scene at all because I feel like I'm not great at capturing real people's likenesses and I don't 'get' the whole 1920s Paris/Stein's salon thing, which is also why Roman Muradov drew the first Hemingway flashback."

But issue 34 was the finale, so Campbell dug in—she knew how important it was to Keatinge. "Looking back on the issue now, I think that part came out pretty good," Campbell says. "I'm still proud of issue 34; it's definitely my favorite one."

Hemingway in *Glory* #34.
By Sophie Campbell.

Hemingway and writer Julio Cortázar square off in this illustration published on August 13, 2013, in the newspaper *La Gaceta* (Tucumán, Argentina). By Ricardo Heredia.

Pesos Pesados (Heavy Weights) (2013)

Here we see Ernest Hemingway and Argentinian writer Julio Cortázar, whose short story "Las babas del diablo" inspired Michelangelo Antonioni's film *Blowup* (1966). One of the founders of the Latin American Boom literary movement, Cortázar—like Hemingway—was a huge fan of boxing.

The two writers square off in an illustration by Ricardo Heredia, published with an essay about writers and boxing for Argentina's *La Gaceta* newspaper.

The piece details the boxing fandom of William Faulkner, Lord Byron, Arthur Conan Doyle, Charles Bukowski, and others. "I was surprised by the number of writers who took boxing as the main subject in some of their novels or tales," says Heredia.

Hemingway, age 16, on February 15, 1916, the year he wrote "A Matter of Colour." Ernest Hemingway Collection. John F. Kennedy Presidential Library and Museum, Boston.

Cover of *The Graphic Canon,* vol. 3, June 2013. © Seven Stories Press.

The Graphic Canon: Volume 3, *From* Heart of Darkness *to* Hemingway *to* Infinite Jest (2013)

In Russ Kick's *Graphic Canon* series, works by classic authors are adapted by modern comic book artists.

Steve Rolston illustrates a piece of journalism that Hemingway wrote for the *Toronto Star,* titled "Living on $1,000 a Year in Paris" (see pp. 133–140, this volume). The panels echo the warmth of Hemingway's posthumous memoir, *A Moveable Feast,* in which he chronicled his life as a struggling writer in Paris, raising a young son with his first wife, Hadley.

"I wished I had died before I ever loved anyone but her," he wrote of Hadley in *A Moveable Feast.*

It would all unravel, however, when Hemingway began to have an affair with their friend Pauline Pfeiffer, a wealthy fashion writer for *Vogue.* He would later marry Pauline, the second of his four wives.

Artist Rolston says that he wasn't "immune to the romantic mystique of Hemingway and the other expat writers living in Paris at that time. That probably drew me to this piece of writing more than anything."

Rolston was also drawn to this adaptation because it was based on a *Toronto Star* story: "As a Canadian, I liked that he was addressing both Americans and my countrymen." An interesting side note: Rolston loves *The Left Bank Gang* (see pp. 73–76 and 81–90, this volume), in which Norwegian cartoonist Jason "reimagines Hemingway, James Joyce, Ezra Pound, and F. Scott Fitzgerald as struggling anthropomorphic cartoonists," Rolston says. "I even gave it a cameo in my comic: there's a boy on the street reading a French edition of Jason's book."

The other Hemingway story in the volume, "A Matter of Colour," was actually written by a teenage Hemingway for his high school literary magazine, the *Tabula.* He appears in Dan Duncan's adaptation as the narrator of this boxing tale, though as the bearded Papa figure of his later years (see pp. 141–146, this volume).

At the time, Duncan was just starting his stint on the *Teenage Mutant Ninja Turtles* for IDW, but the chance to bring the story to light proved too good to pass up. "I love Hemingway's work and, at the time, there was a lack of comics adapting it, AND it had boxing! So I was hooked," Duncan says.

He chose to make the narrator an elder Hemingway—rather than a high school student—for clarity. "I personally know Hemingway as older, and slightly grizzled. Just like I know Hunter S. Thompson as balding, with teashades and a cigarette holder. Or Stan Lee with a mustache," Duncan says. "And I just didn't think I could pull off a high school student and still evoke 'Hemingway.'"

It's also worth noting that when Hemingway originally published this story, classmate Elmore Brown provided some illustrations.

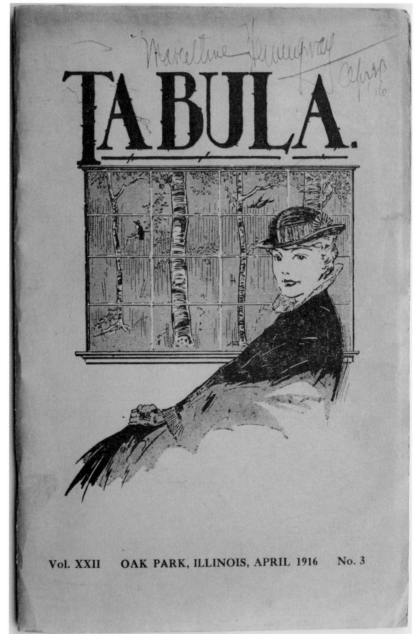

Top, left and right: Illustrations from "A Matter of Colour" page in the *Tabula.* Courtesy Oak Park Public Library.

Left: April 1916 issue of Oak Park and River Forest High School's literary magazine, the *Tabula,* which included Hemingway's "A Matter of Colour." This is the personal copy of Hemingway's older sister Marcelline. Photo by Robert K. Elder from the collection of the Oak Park Public Library.

Following pages: Panels of Hemingway's *Toronto Star* piece adapted by comic book artist Steve Rolston. Courtesy Steve Rolston. Reprinted with permission.

Living on $1000 a Year in Paris

WRITTEN BY ERNEST HEMINGWAY
ILLUSTRATED BY STEVE ROLSTON

Paris in the winter is rainy, cold, beautiful and cheap.

It is also noisy, jostling, crowded and cheap.

It is anything you want -- and cheap.

The dollar, either Canadian or American, is the key to Paris.

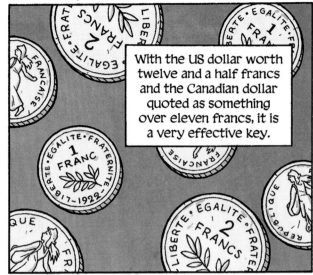

With the US dollar worth twelve and a half francs and the Canadian dollar quoted as something over eleven francs, it is a very effective key.

At the present rate of exchange, a Canadian with an income of one thousand dollars a year can live comfortably and enjoyably in Paris.

If exchange were normal, the same Canadian would starve to death.

Exchange is a wonderful thing.

Two of us are living in a comfortable hotel in the Rue Jacob, it is just back of the Academy of the Beaux Arts and a few minutes' walk from the Tuileries.

Our room costs twelve francs a day for two.

It is clean, light, well heated, has hot and cold running water and a bathroom on the same floor.

That makes a cost for rent of thirty dollars a month.

SIZZLE
SIZZLE

Breakfast costs us both two francs and a half.

That totals seventy-five francs a month, or about six dollars and three or four cents.

BISTRO Le Pré aux Clercs BRASSERIE

LE PRÉ AUX CLERCS

CAFÉ

At the corner of the Rue Bonaparte and the Rue Jacob there is a splendid restaurant where the prices are a la carte.

Soups cost sixty centimes, and a fish is 1.20 francs.

The meals are roast beef, veal cutlet, lamb, mutton and thick steaks served with potatoes prepared as only the French can cook them.

These cost 2.40 francs an order.

Brussels sprouts in butter, creamed spinach, beans, sifted peas and cauliflower vary in price from forty to eighty-five centimes.

Desserts are seventy-five centimes and sometimes as much as a franc.

Salad is sixty centimes.

Red wine is sixty centimes a bottle and beer is forty centimes a glass.

My wife and I have an excellent meal there, equal in cooking and quality of food to the best restaurants in America, for fifty cents apiece.

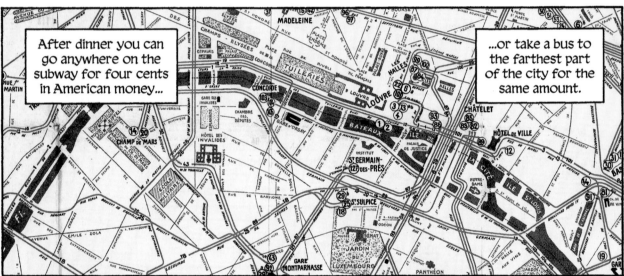

After dinner you can go anywhere on the subway for four cents in American money...

...or take a bus to the farthest part of the city for the same amount.

It sounds unbelievable but it is simply a case of prices not having advanced in proportion to the increased value of the dollar.

All of Paris is not so cheap, however, for the big hotels located around the Opera and the Madeline are more expensive than ever.

We ran into two girls from New York the other day in the Luxembourg Gardens.

All of us crossed on the same boat, and they had gone to one of the big, highly-advertised hotels.

Their rooms were costing them sixty francs a day apiece, and other charges in proportion.

For two days and three nights at their hotel, they received a bill for five hundred francs, or forty-two dollars.

They are now located in a hotel on the left bank of the Seine, where five hundred francs will last two weeks instead of two days...

...and are as comfortable as they were at the tourist hotel.

It is from tourists who stop at the large hotels that the reports come that living in Paris is very high.

The big hotelkeepers charge all they think the traffic can bear.

But there are several hundred small hotels in all parts of Paris...

...where an American or Canadian can live comfortably...

...eat at attractive restaurants...

...and find amusement...

...for a total expenditure of two and one half to three dollars a day.

Originally published in the Toronto Star newspaper on February 4, 1922.

THE TORONTO DAILY STAR

NEW RULES OF WARFARE PLANNED BY NATIO

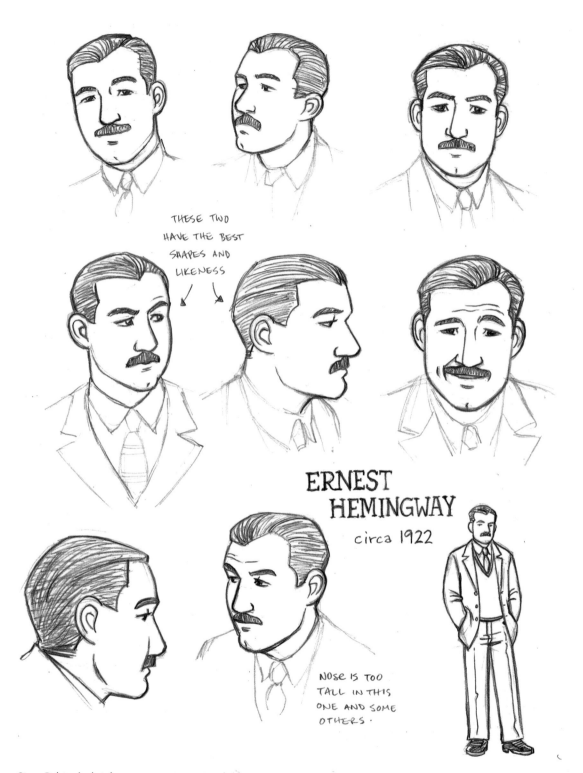

THESE TWO HAVE THE BEST SHAPES AND LIKENESS

ERNEST HEMINGWAY

circa 1922

NOSE IS TOO TALL IN THIS ONE AND SOME OTHERS.

Steve Rolston's sketches of Hemingway.

Facing and following pages: Dan Duncan's adaptation of Hemingway's "A Matter of Colour." Courtesy Dan Duncan.

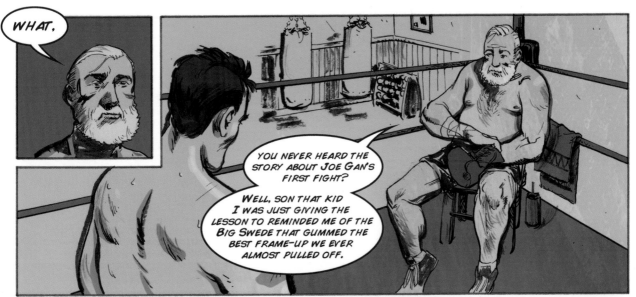

WHAT,

YOU NEVER HEARD THE STORY ABOUT JOE GAN'S FIRST FIGHT?

WELL, SON THAT KID I WAS JUST GIVING THE LESSON TO REMINDED ME OF THE BIG SWEDE THAT GUMMED THE BEST FRAME-UP WE EVER ALMOST PULLED OFF.

THE YARN'S A CLASSIC NOW; BUT I'LL GIVE IT TO YOU JUST AS IT HAPPENED.

ALONG BACK IN 1902 I WAS MANAGING A SORT OF A NEW LIGHTWEIGHT BY THE NAME OF MONTANA DAN MORGAN.

WELL, THIS DAN PERSON WAS ONE OF THOSE ROUGH AND READY LADS, GAME AND ALL THAT, BUT WITH NO FOOT-WORK,

BUT WITH A KICK LIKE A MULE IN HIS RIGHT FIN,

BUT WITH A WEAK LEFT THAT WOULDN'T DENT MELTED BUTTER.

I'D GOTTEN ALONG PRETTY WELL WITH THE BIRD,

AND WE'D COLLECTED SUNDRY SHEKELS

FIGHTING DOCKWALLOPERS AND STEVEDORES AND PRELIMINARY BOYS OUT AT THE OLD OLYMPIC CLUB.

OLYMPIC CLUB

DAN WAS GETTING TO BE QUITE A SIZABLE SCRAPPER,

AND BY USING HIS STRONG RIGHT MITT AND STALLING ALONG, HE MANAGED TO ACHIEVE QUITE A REPUTATION.

DAN MORGAN VS JIM O'ROURKE
20 Rounds
OLYMPIC
MORGAN   SEATS $2   O'ROURKE
FRIDAY 8 PM

SO I MATCHED THE LAD WITH JIM O'ROURKE, THE OLD TRIAL HORSE,

AND THE BOY MANAGED TO HANG ONE ON JIM'S JAW THAT WAS GOOD FOR THE TEN-SECOND ANESTHETIC.

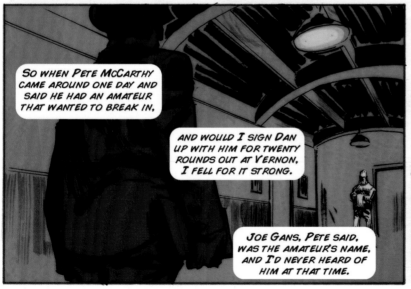

SO WHEN PETE McCARTHY CAME AROUND ONE DAY AND SAID HE HAD AN AMATEUR THAT WANTED TO BREAK IN,

AND WOULD I SIGN DAN UP WITH HIM FOR TWENTY ROUNDS OUT AT VERNON, I FELL FOR IT STRONG.

JOE GANS, PETE SAID, WAS THE AMATEUR'S NAME, AND I'D NEVER HEARD OF HIM AT THAT TIME.

I THOUGHT THAT IT WAS KIND OF STRANGE WHEN PETE CAME AROUND WITH A CONTRACT THAT HAD A $500 FORFEIT CLAUSE IN IT FOR NON-APPEARANCE,

BUT WE INTENDED TO APPEAR ALRIGHT, SO I SIGNED UP.

'BOB, TAKE A LOOK AT THIS HAND.'

WELL, WE DIDN'T TRAIN MUCH FOR THE SCRAP, AND TWO DAYS BEFORE IT WAS TO COME OFF, DAN COMES UP TO ME AND SAYS:

HOLY SMOKES! DANNY, WHERE DID YOU GET THAT?

THE BAG BUSTED LOOSE WHILE I WAS PUNCHIN' IT

AND ME RIGHT BANGED INTO THE FRAMEWORK.

WELL, YOU'VE DONE IT NOW, I YELPED. THERE'S THAT 500 IRON MEN IN THE FORFEIT, AND I'VE PUT DOWN EVERYTHING I'VE GOT ON YOU TO WIN BY K.O.

'BOB,' SAYS DANNY. 'I'VE GOT A SCHEME.'

YOU KNOW THE WAY THE RING IS OUT THERE AT THE OLYMPIC? UP ON THE STAGE WITH THAT OLD CLOTH DROP CURTAIN IN THE BACK?

WELL, IN THE FIRST ROUND, BEFORE THEY FIND OUT ABOUT THIS BAD FLIPPER OF MINE, I'LL RUSH THE SMOKE UP AGAINST THE CURTAIN

(YOU KNOW JOE GANS WAS A "PUSSON OF COLOR")

AND YOU HAVE SOMEBODY BACK THERE WITH A BASEBALL BAT, AND SWAT HIM ON THE HEAD FROM BEHIND THE CURTAIN.

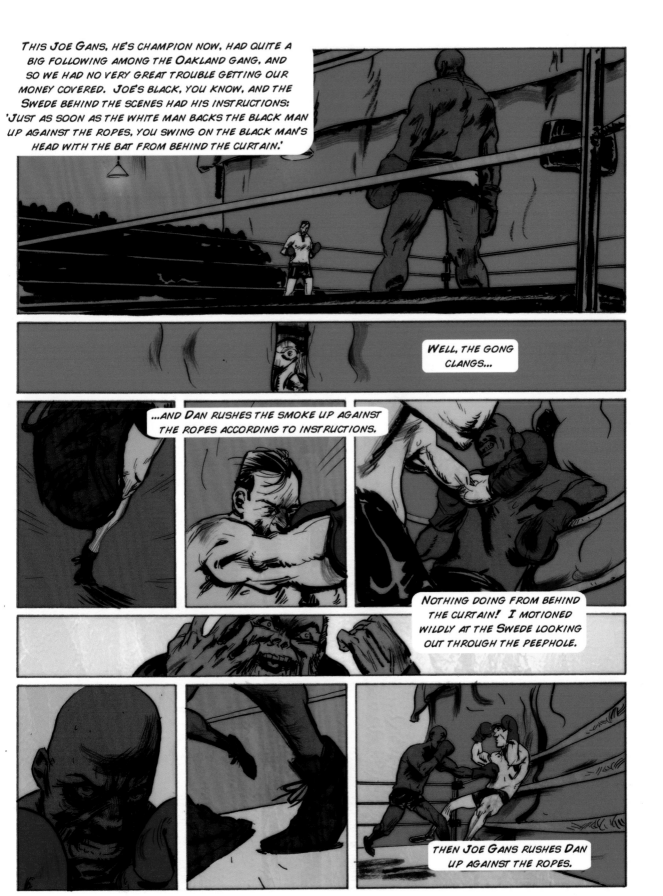

COMES A CRACK AND DAN DROPS LIKE A POLED OVER OX.

HOLY SMOKE! THE SWEDE HAD HIT THE WRONG MAN! ALL OUR KALE WAS GONE!

I CLIMBED INTO THE RING, GRABBED DAN AND DRAGGED HIM INTO THE DRESSING ROOM BY THE FEET. THERE WASN'T ANY NEED FOR THE REFEREE TO COUNT TEN; HE MIGHT HAVE COUNTED 300.

THERE WAS THE SWEDE. "I LIT INTO HIM: 'YOU MISERABLE APOLOGY FOR A LOW-GRADE IMBECILE!

YOU EVIDENCE OF GOD'S CARELESSNESS! WHY IN THE NAME OF THE PROPHET DID YOU HIT THE WHITE MAN INSTEAD OF THE BLACK MAN?'

MISTER ARMSTRONG,'HE SAYS, 'YOU NO SHOULD TALK AT ME LIKE THAT – I BANE COLOR BLIND!'

Superzelda: The Graphic Life of Zelda Fitzgerald (2013)

Hemingway and Zelda Fitzgerald, the wife of F. Scott Fitzgerald, disliked one another deeply. Zelda thought Hemingway was a phony, and Hemingway considered her a bad influence who contributed to Scott's alcoholism and his eventual inability to write.

Artist Daniele Marotta and writer Tiziana Lo Porto were working on a comics column for *D–la Repubblica delle donne,* the Saturday magazine of the Italian newspaper *La Repubblica.* They used the page to review contemporary novels, and one week in 2008 they critiqued Gilbert Leroy's *Alabama Song,* a fictionalized account of Zelda Fitzgerald's life.

"And we both fell in love with Zelda," says Lo Porto. "I started reading about her, and I discovered that Scott Fitzgerald was the only one who honestly portrayed Zelda."

Writer Tiziana Lo Porto thought that Hemingway's portrayal of Zelda as a jealous, unsupportive wife was both unfair and false, so she set out to correct the historical record.

Cover of *Superzelda,* a graphic novel that features a Zelda Fitzgerald who is different from Hemingway's portrayal of her.

Lo Porto continues: "Scott and Zelda were truly in love, and tried their best to help each other. Zelda helped enormously. . . . She didn't want to be a writer, although she wrote a great novel and some great short stories and articles. Mostly she wanted to be the heroine of her beloved husband's novels (that's the reason why she married him)."

Hemingway does show up, however tangentially, in Zelda's tale.

The title of the graphic novel was an inside joke that stuck, remembers artist Daniele Marotta: "*Superzelda* was the production name, as we perceived Zelda as a superhero. In the end, we saw the strong pop entity that the book had become, so we called it *Superzelda* for real."

Hemingway in *Superzelda*. Courtesy Tiziana
Lo Porto and Daniele Marotta, 2013.

Educational Poster #36: Alcoholic Authors (2013)

Artist Aaron Bagley primarily uses this image as a portfolio piece on his website, though he's made postcards and tote bags from it.

"It's part of my educational poster series," Bagley says. "Each one is different from the next—culinary stars, punk rock singers, et cetera. The piece was inspired by my time spent working around books. I was a library assistant in art school, and after I graduated I eventually became staff at a used bookshop."

Although Hemingway isn't a particular favorite, Bagley says that he's drawn to the circle of artists and authors Hemingway made friends with in Paris. "The Lost Generation has an appeal that continues to intrigue generation after generation. Their personal lives also provide interest as

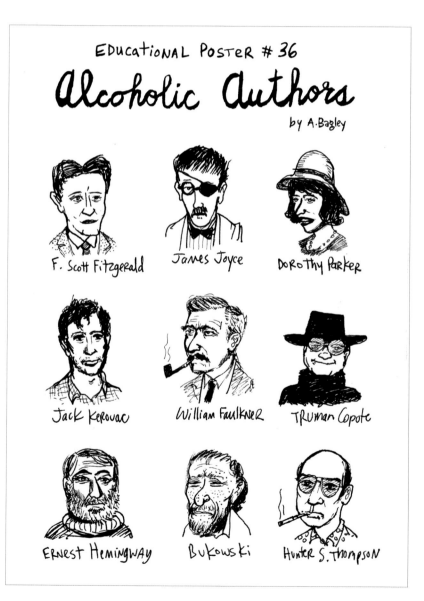

Hemingway in *Educational Poster #36: Alcoholic Authors*, 2013. © Aaron Bagley. Reprinted with permission of the artist. All rights reserved. Aaronbagley.com.

the different authors mingled with each other and that provides a sort of mystery worth exploring historically or in fictional works," Bagley says. "It's a romantic setting for artists to daydream about and wish to be a part of. Personally, I am drawn to any group of artists where ideas are bouncing around and colleagues are helping one another out."

If you look closely, you might spot a typo.

"Yes, there is a spelling error that I did not correct, because I enjoy when people are quick enough to spot it. This is a common theme in my work—I leave mistakes as a way to make it more human. Something I hope Hemingway would appreciate."

Ernest Hemingway (2013)

Ric Stultz's portfolio piece is part of his series of his "favorite deceased creators." Other figures in the series include Billie Holiday, Jim Henson, Francis Bacon, and Tupac Shakur.

"Hemingway is one of my favorite authors, I've read all his books, some multiple times," says Stultz, a Wisconsin-based illustrator who has done work for Nike, MTV, and YouTube. "*To Have and Have Not* is a personal favorite."

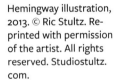

Hemingway illustration, 2013. © Ric Stultz. Reprinted with permission of the artist. All rights reserved. Studiostultz. com.

He continues: "I like that it takes place in Florida; he rarely wrote about America. He's so tied to Key West in the American psyche, but this is his only book that takes place there. It's also morally ambiguous. The main character is a bit of an antihero. It also changes perspective a bunch, so you get a look inside the character's head and then a view of what the rest of the world thinks of him."

Stultz chose this 1950s-era *Life* magazine Hemingway rather than the iconic beard-and-sweater version because he "really just liked the look in his eye and his big mustache. At this point he looks world weary but still empathetic. When looking for photos to reference I came across several from this period in his life and they most resonated with me. It's a graying middle-aged Hemingway, his best is behind him but he's not yet to *The Old Man and the Sea*."

The cover of *Life* magazine, September 1, 1952, courtesy of the Oak Park Public Library's Hemingway Archives, owned by the Ernest Hemingway Foundation of Oak Park.

Hemingway's image—and work—survives because "good art survives, and Hemingway is the best," Stultz says. "He's a masculine writer but has a lot of empathy in his work, that's a rare mix. He's also an extremely great writer, the man didn't waste words, everything was to the point. He had seen a lot of the good and the bad of the world, and he combined it in compact prose."

Moral Formation and Graphic Adaptations of Hemingway's Works

Sean C. Hadley

Introduction

What makes something a bad adaptation? Is it a deviation from the source material that the audience repudiates? Conversely, is an adaptation bad if those adapting a work earn the ire of the audience but are applauded by the original author? Or is it simply an issue of quality, as Hemingway often faced when his works were adapted into film? Whatever the case, adapting a work is a dangerous business. This is perhaps truer in the world of comic books and graphic novels than in any other media today. Comics, after all, are the corrupters of youth, the childhood memory that is best left in a dusty box, stored somewhere in the attic.[1] Do graphic novel adaptations of classic works fit into this same category? Perhaps a graphic novel adaptation of *Beowulf* would fare better than the box office failures that have made their way to DVDs in the last two decades? Just as the films based on canonical stories tend to be a mixed bag, the same goes in the world of graphic novels. But as G. K. Chesterton observed over a century ago, there are "treasures" in the "dust-heaps of humanity." Even those things often denigrated in the press or in popular outrage online are worth an investigation to see exactly what they contain and what jewels might be found among the wreckage. In that way, not much has changed since the proliferation of penny dreadfuls. And just as those publications were once the "actual centre of a million flaming imaginations," graphic novels act as catalysts for the minds of many today.[2] And given the proliferation of Ernest Hemingway's appearances in comic books and films, it is worth wondering whether his own works ought to be adapted into the graphic novel form or whether such adaptations are successful.

Aristotle's Categories

Adaptations are as old as Aristotle, at the very least. A quick look through the ancient Greek and Roman writers is enough to show just how important it is to reimagine established stories. The works of Sophocles, Aeschylus, and Ovid all prompt specific factors to consider regarding which stories are preserved and, perhaps more important, why they are preserved. Aristotle's *Poetics* is still the easiest and most succinct guide to this end. The format lends itself readily to critical thinking and analysis, and Aristotle's insights continue to be relevant to the modern reader. His six elements remain crucial in the interpretation of any good story; one readily recognizes the importance of "plot-structure, character, style, thought, spectacle, lyric poetry" and their modern counterparts in the publishing world of graphic novels, even if they do not quite get it at first.[3] It is a common assumption that spectacle drives a comic book, but it is not too difficult to demonstrate why, even in the graphic novel world, spectacle will only get a story so far. Consider the short-lived independent publishing houses like WildStorm and Top Cow Comics, which were home to comics that were beautifully drawn but had less than engaging characters and plots. Though these comics attracted attention initially, titles such as *Supreme* and *Cyberforce* lost readership as the plots gravitated toward hackneyed tropes and weak dialogue. Such will not keep the attention of the reading public for long unless it is coupled with plot and character development. Comic creators do not always see eye to eye on this, but the issue is something at the forefront in the minds of artists and writers. Erik Larsen, creator of *Savage Dragon*, describes his creative process as "story driven," noting that even his panel decisions "depend on the story."[4] But even major publishers sometimes experiment with these categories, such as the Marvel Comics wordless "'Nuff Said" month in 2002.[5] It is no surprise that the experiment has not been repeated. Spectacle cannot carry a comic book alone.

For the character to be second to the plot may strike one as odd, but only initially. One need not read Hemingway's work long to begin realizing the necessity of a structured novel, even when it does not fit a stereotypical plotline. Think of *In Our Time*'s vignettes that, devoid of a typical plot, further build the artistic development of the collection as a whole. Such a work seems to cry out for a visual adaptation. This is not to diminish the role of the individual in any story. Aristotle's analysis of *Oedipus Tyrannus* hinges upon his understanding of the man, Oedipus.[6] Through elements such as thought and speech, an author develops the character, but ought to allow plot to guide this development. Hemingway's fiction provides a modern example of this same idea, as dialogue and inner thoughts are sparse throughout the text, so that readers "glimpse the inner life of the characters only obliquely."[7] It is action that drives development, as speech is reserved for only the most essential revelations, as with Nick Adams in "Indian Camp." When "Three Shots" serves as an introduction, Nick's spiritual crisis becomes more explicit, while the removal of that context leaves the reader to ascertain from the movement of the story what is going on between Nick and his father.[8] While each element gives readers the right language and concepts toward understanding a graphic novel, it is important to remember that Aristotle saw these as part of a hierarchy, with "the structure of events" at the top "while spectacle . . . is the least integral of all to the poet's art."[9] This can, and perhaps should, be used as a tool for examining a work's adaptation. Why might an artist or director include more spectacle and less plot? Any drastic shifts in Aristotle's hierarchy ought to offer a justification for these changes, something that must be understandable from the work itself.

In addition to these basic categories, Aristotle's *Poetics* also provides more than technical points with which to understand a visual adaptation of any given work, mainly by his insistence upon the moral formation of the audience, which takes place through the audience's participation in katharsis and mimesis. Though these terms are somewhat debated, *katharsis* is used here as an emotional release that has an effect on one's ethical dispositions, whereas *mimesis* is thought of as the basic relation between art and the world, including its imitative qualities.[10] Together, these concepts attempt to help the audience understand what the artist is accomplishing. The point is a simple one: stories teach ethics. This is true of graphic novels and comic books, though such media forms are often associated with entertainment. Binge-watching Netflix shows has shifted the way audiences consider moral formation and serial adaptations, with Gen Y and Gen Z seemingly more attuned to certain ethical concerns.[11] Such habits might acknowledge the moral origins of a story, evidenced by Disney's warning on its recent streaming service, that some content might contain "outdated cultural depictions."[12] But the idea that these stories are formative appears less tenable from this perspective focused on potential offense. In the abstract, a story is meant to entertain or to affirm the emotions the audience is already experiencing. But for Aristotle, stories are a confrontation. Even his categories of comedy and tragedy find their anchors in a moral understanding of the world. For comedy to represent humanity at its worst, or tragedy humanity at its best, readers must be willing to interpret the world around them and be confronted by what they discover. It is not as simple as labeling this "good" and that "bad," however. According to the German philosopher Hans-Georg Gadamer, "moral knowledge, as Aristotle describes it, is clearly not objective knowledge—that is the knower is not standing over against a situation that he merely observes; he is directly confronted with what he sees. It is something that he has to do."[13] Every work of literature, then, acts as a declaration, a demand to be evaluated. This is where comics are particularly unique; the graphic novel is a dynamic visual presentation but not in the sense of performance. The graphic novel offers a valuable in-between space where the source material is transformed. While it is not exactly what Aristotle had in mind 2,300 years ago, his theory holds remarkably true when analyzing the moral formation on display in the world of comics. And therefore, the pairing of Hemingway with graphic novels is fruitful for study, for it opens up a special lens toward reading the moral layers of Hemingway's great works.

The Graphic Adaptations

Crucial in this discussion is the recognition that at their core, Hemingway's works are moral treatises. H. R. Stoneback, Larry Grimes, and Allen Josephs have all written extensively about this over the last four decades. Josephs encourages readers to see the "moral, spiritual, even ecstatic dimension" of something like *The Sun Also Rises,* and recognizing this helps to see these patterns in Hemingway's other works as well.[14] But this connection also bridges the gap with Aristotle's *Poetics* in interpreting Hemingway's writing. If Aristotle is correct, what implications might this moral approach to reading have for the works of Ernest Hemingway? This question, I would say, is one that ought to linger in the mind before, during, and after reading Hemingway's corpus. Not only will it aid readers in understanding Hemingway's writing patterns, it will assist them in grappling with the many adaptations of Hemingway's work.

The graphic novel allows for certain advantages in terms of adaptation, making it superior in many ways for addressing interpretive issues, especially if an artist is attempting to represent the work's moral value. Philip Sidney is helpful here as well: "Poesy, therefore, is an art of imitation; for so Aristotle termeth it in the word μίμησις; that is to say, a representing, counterfeiting, or figuring forth: to speak metaphorically, *a speaking picture;* with this end, to teach and delight."[15] Comics are valuable especially since they embody this concept—namely, speaking pictures. Of course, this avenue of study is not without its troubles. It should be noted up front that the selections are indeed sparse when one attempts to study how Hemingway's works have been adapted into the graphic novel form.[16] Of note, there are merely two adaptations found in Russ Kick's *The Graphic Canon,* volume 3 (see pp. 129–130 and 133–146, this volume). He includes lesser-known pieces from Hemingway's oeuvre because, simply put, they are some of the only ones in print. Though both pieces are clearly Hemingway in tone, they lack the style and iceberg quality that would characterize his later work.[17] Analyzing these two pieces alongside their source material still bears fruitful study; such an analysis can move the reader farther, faster into the moral realm of Hemingway's writing.

One Hemingway story in Kick's arrangement is "A Matter of Colour," adapted by Dan Duncan. This piece is based on a short story Hemingway wrote in high school, which has garnered occasional attention.[18] Still, its early manifestations of Hemingway's action writing, as well as its terse dialogue, make it a reasonable choice for adaptation. Not only does the story stylistically work well with Aristotle's categories, but the context for the story provides further moral formation. Much of Hemingway's punch line here stems from the 1908 boxing match between Jack Johnson and Stanley Ketchel. As all of Jack Johnson's fights with white boxers brought race tensions to the surface, his almost defeat at Ketchel's hands fanned the flames that led to the 1910 fight between Johnson and Jim Jeffries. Yet Hemingway's story was not published until 1916, when Johnson had lost his boxing title and fled to Europe under the threat of arrest.[19] Hemingway captures all of this tension in the closing lines of "A Matter of Colour": "'Why in the name of the Prophet did you hit the white man instead of the black man?' 'Mister Armstrong,' he says, 'you no should talk at me like that—I bane color blind.'"[20] Even at this early stage in his writing, Hemingway was playing action and concision to tackle ethical situations, occasionally in a humorous form.

After reading the story by itself, the reader can easily recognize two things in the graphic adaptation: the art has a grainy feel and the coach is clearly an elderly Hemingway. This second aspect might catch a reader off guard, especially in light of Aristotle's thoughts on character. The visual addition of the original author creates a sort of feedback that colors the reading. From there, it is well to ask questions about the artwork. "What adjectives fit this particular style?" Gritty. Sketch art. Angry. "What sort of stories might one associate with it?" Perhaps it is reminiscent of boxing films or other such movies from the first half of the twentieth century? "Which of Aristotle's elements seems most prominent in this adaptation?" The art, particularly during the fight scene, takes on a sense of the spectacle, and it can be a challenge to take note of anything else. This very serious style of art jars the reader away from what ought to be humorous, given that this specific story that hangs on the final punch line. Here it can be seen how spectacle takes away from the plot and dialogue, treating what is comedic as something more in the tragic mode. The bottom left panel on the last page shows an enraged-looking Hemingway waving his finger at the botched attempt to cheat.[21] This serves as a kind of touchstone to the assessment. Certainly, the Hemingway short story is an early attempt at humor, but this point becomes befuddled when the artist inserts the author into the piece, accompanied by an overly serious art style.

Another Hemingway story in this volume of *The Graphic Canon* is a short piece of journalism titled "Living on $1,000 a Year in Paris," adapted by Steve Rolston. While no major collection includes the article, it is a part of the *Toronto Star*'s Hemingway Papers and is readily accessible at the *Star*'s website.[22] It helps that these two adaptations are completely different in approach and tone. Of course, as seems to be the pattern of artists in such instances, Hemingway makes a cameo. But given the nature of journalism, perhaps this character intrusion can be forgiven. "What does the use of color suggest about this adaptation?" It reminds the reader of newspapers, or of films associated with Paris in the twenties. "How does the mixture of abstract and concrete imagery change one's reading of the article?" The astute reader might be quick to appreciate how the images enhance what seems an otherwise plotless piece of writing; the visual element allows the reader to see the "story" in Hemingway's journalism. However, readers might also find the addition of maps and scales to detract from this, bringing in a sort of spectacle that distorts what was otherwise beginning to take a positive shape.[23] The addition of the topless dancer at the end of the comic ought to strike one as especially odd, even if the reader likes the effect it has on the article. In this case, spectacle comes in a muted tone but dominates the meaning of the story once it becomes involved. While initially a way to provide plot and character into a journalistic piece devoid of both, spectacle falls too quickly into the same abstraction that makes the writing difficult to adapt on its own.

Given their early date in Hemingway's career, it might be tempting to dismiss the moral formation of these stories Yet, there are the necessary elements here for examination, even if germinal. While the pieces are some of Hemingway's lighter fare, both provide insight into themes worth further discussion. Racism may be a laughing matter at the end of Hemingway's early short fiction, but if one bears in mind Bill's progressive stance toward the African American boxer, it is a reasonable connection to make. Though a product of his context, Hemingway does not easily fit the racist narrative sometimes foisted upon him. This is missing in Duncan's adaptation of "A Matter of Colour," and it is not hard for readers to recognize this loss in moral impetus. Likewise, the concept of living well, another aspect that permeates *The Sun Also Rises,* finds expression in "Living on $1,000 a Year in Paris." Jake embodies the frugality seen in Hemingway's short article in a way that the journalism does not necessarily capture, but that almost manages to emerge in the graphic novel adaptation. However, it is impossible for the cartoonish qualities of Rolston's abstract additions to compete with the esoteric, but grounded, conversations between Jake and Count Mippipopolous.[24] Even when the illustrations are helpful, something seems to be missing in this important moral element of Hemingway's work. The reader might be left asking: "What is missing?" And the answer seems to be Hemingway's artistic ethic.

By Comparison

Still, it is not as though every classic story adapted into a graphic novel fails to meet Aristotle's criteria. Though Kick's compilation shows that there exists a vast number of retellings in this graphic format, it would be impossible to cover them all in such a limited space. But it is a good idea to look at an example that understands the meaning of the source material, balancing the visual and written elements. And perhaps the best instance of this, and the one most easily recognizable beforehand, is F. Scott Fitzgerald's "The Curious Case of Benjamin Button."[25] Many readers will be more familiar with the movie, with some even unaware that it

Illustration from the graphic adaptation of Fitzgerald's "The Curious Case of Benjamin Button." Kevin Cornell, 2013.

is based on a Fitzgerald tale. Fitzgerald's work lacks the iceberg quality of Hemingway's writing, which, in one sense, makes it easier to adapt. Benjamin Button's birth illustrates this point quite well. Readers would be justified to laugh aloud as they read: "The old man turned wearily to the nurse. 'Nice way to welcome a new-born child,' he complained in a weak voice. 'Tell him he's wrong, why don't you?'"[26] The humor is inescapable when one thinks of a grumpy old man giving voice to such a common experience for so many children, but here the tone is reversed through Button's curmudgeonly demeanor. And this scene takes on the same sense of humor, if not a heightened one, in its comic adaptation. Button's knees protruding ridiculously from his tiny crib adds to the character's growth rather than devolving into mere spectacle, and the visuals continually confirm the character development just as Fitzgerald described. Aristotle's genre breakdown works well here, with comedy, tragedy, and reality serving as reminders of what a story is communicating.[27]

Perhaps due to Fitzgerald's superficial narrative, or maybe because of the adapters' grasp of the source material and its meaning, *The Curious Case of Benjamin Button* positively illustrates these Aristotelian categories. This comparison helps to show how Aristotle's thinking can enhance the reading of a graphic novel, as well as detract from it. Kevin Cornell's artistic style balances well with the age of Fitzgerald without trying to glamorize what is a comical story.

Conclusion

The sense that there is some aspect of Hemingway's work that makes it obscure—or worse, something that makes it unadaptable—permeates discussions of adaptations of his novels and short stories. Hemingway's works have staying power because in them people do learn to see beyond what is only on the surface, as he stated in his letter to Bernard Berenson regarding *The Old Man and the Sea*.[28] And this sort of exercise drives the point home in an emphatic way. It is appropriate for a reader to begin asking, "Where did Rolston get the idea of using a map?" (And an answer may very well be found in *The Sun Also Rises*.) If readers ask these sorts of questions, they will soon find themselves digging deeper and deeper into the layers of Hemingway's work. The additional art form gives depth to what already seems an unfathomable task. And in this light, I would suggest that Hemingway's works ought to be adapted. On the screen, on the stage, and on the colored page. The layers of meaning in Ernest Hemingway's writing may find an appropriate expression through the graphic novel. Why should Joyce and Fitzgerald have all the fun? Hopefully, by combining an Aristotelian lens and the modernist fascination with understatement, readers might just find that graphic novels offer more than artwork, something other than what could be described as merely "pretty."

Notes

1. When Fredric Wertham's *Seduction of the Innocent* (New York: Rhinehart & Company) was released in 1954, there was a palpable sense in which comics earned the ire of many adults. Consider how much things have changed, when Bradford Wright's *Comic Book Nation: The Transformation of Youth Culture in America* (Baltimore: John Hopkins Univ. Press) claimed in 2003 that the "Death of Superman" storyline was "a powerful metaphor for American culture and the comic-book industry in the post–Cold War era" (282).

2. G. K. Chesterton, "In Defence of Penny Dreadfuls," *The Defendant* (London: J. M. Dent & Company, 1907), 6. 8.

3. *The Poetics of Aristotle,* trans. Stephen Halliwell (Chapel Hill: Univ. of North Carolina Press, 1987), 37.

4. Jeffery Klaehn, "'The Important Thing, Always, Is to Tell a Good Story': An Interview with Comic Book Creator Erik Larsen," *Journal of Graphic Novels and Comics* 7, no. 4 (2016): 449.

5. All of the issues included in this experiment were collected and reissued in a trade paperback, Grant Morrison and J. Michael Straczynski's *'Nuff Said* (New York: Marvel Comics, 2002).

6. Aristotle, *Poetics,* 154–55.

7. Zaidi Ali Shehzad, "The Camouflage of the Sacred in Hemingway's Short Fiction," *Theory in Action* 7 (Apr. 2014): 104–20.

8. For a thorough analysis of how "Three Shots" changes the interpretation of "Indian Camp," see Donald Daiker, "In Defense of Hemingway's Doctor Adams: The Case for 'Indian Camp,'" *Hemingway Review* 35, no. 2 (Spring 2016): 55–61.

9. Aristotle, *Poetics,* 37–38.

10. Aristotle, *Poetics,* 37, 44.

11. Sidneyeve Matrix, "The Netflix Effect: Teens, Binge Watching, and On-Demand Digital Media Trends," *Jeunesse: Young People, Texts, Cultures* 6, no. 1 (2014): 120.

12. Ben Arnold, "Disney+ Provides On-Screen Warnings to Viewers over 'Outdated Cultural Depictions,'" *Yahoo Movies UK,* Nov. 14, 2019, https://news.yahoo.com/disney-provides-warning-to-viewers-over-outdated-cultural-depictions-084348034.html.

13. Hans-George Gadamer, *Truth and Method,* trans. Joel Weinsheimer and Donald G. Marshall (1975; repr., New York: Bloomsbury Academic, 2013), 362.

14. Allen Josephs, "Toreo: The Moral Axis of *The Sun Also Rises,*" *On Hemingway and Spain: Essays and Reviews, 1979–2013* (Wickford, RI: New Street Communications, 2014), 140.

15. Philip Sidney, *The Defence of Poesy,* in *The Library of the Old English Prose Writers,* vol. 2 of 9, ed. Alexander Young (Cambridge: Hillard & Brown, 1831), 15, emphasis added.

16. Theirry Murat's *Il vecchio e il mare* (*The Old Man and the Sea*) is a notable exception but is only available in Italian. One might also consider the animated short film adaptation of *The Old Man and the Sea* by Aleksandr Petrov as a possible exception as well, since it is largely stop-motion animation. Though available in English, it is difficult to get a copy. That both of these other options are adaptations of *The Old Man and the Sea* is not coincidental; the story of Santiago is Hemingway's highpoint in terms of blending moral formation and literary aesthetics.

17. Ernest Hemingway, *Death in the Afternoon* (1932; repr., New York: Scribner's, 1995), 192.

18. This story is printed rarely and was left out of the 2017 addition to Scribner's Hemingway's Library Editions, *The Short Stories of Ernest Hemingway* edited by Seán Hemingway, this even though two of the young Hemingway's stories were included over "A Matter of Colour."

19. Gregory Green, "'A Matter of Color': Hemingway's Criticism of Race Prejudice," *Hemingway Review* 1 (Fall 1981): 28–29.

20. Ernest Hemingway. "A Matter of Colour." *Ernest Hemingway's Apprenticeship: Oak Park, 1916–1917,* ed. Matthew J. Bruccoli (Columbia, SC: Bruccoli-Clark Layman, 1972), 101.

21. Dan Duncan, adaptation of "A Matter of Colour," in *The Graphic Canon:* vol. 3, *From Heart of Darkness to Hemingway to Infinite Jest,* ed. Russ Kick (New York: Seven Stories Press, 2013), 139, 144.

22. Ernest Hemingway, "A Canadian with $1,000 a Year Can Live Very Comfortably and Enjoyably in Paris," *Toronto Star Weekly,* Feb. 4, 1922, http://ehto.thestar.com/marks/a-canadian-with-1000-a-year-can-live-very-comfortably-and-enjoyably-in-paris.

23. Steve Rolston, adaptation, "Living on $1,000 a Year in Paris," in Kick, *Graphic Canon,* 251, 255.

24. Ernest Hemingway, *The Sun Also Rises: The Hemingway Library Edition,* ed. Seán Hemingway (New York: Scribner, 2014), 58–59, 46–53.

25. It is worth noting that this adaptation was released close to the film's debut, which starred Brad Pitt in the titular role. The film version offers an appalling interpretation of Fitzgerald's humor, exchanging the comedy for a tragedy of the worst kind.

26. F. Scott Fitzgerald, "The Curious Case of Benjamin Button," *The Short Stories of F. Scott Fitzgerald* (New York: Scribner's, 1989), 160, 164.

27. F. Scott Fitzgerald, *The Curious Case of Benjamin Button: A Graphic Novel,* adapted by Nunzio DeFilippis and Christina Weir and illustrated by Kevin Cornell (New York: Quirk Books, 2008), 18, 36.

28. Ernest Hemingway to Bernard Berenson, Sept. 13, 1952, *Selected Letters: 1917–1961,* ed. Carlos Baker (New York: Scribner's, 1981), 780.

2014–2019

Hemingway at Sea, in the Afterlife, and Beyond

Nathan Hale's Hazardous Tales: Treaties, Trenches, Mud, and Blood (A World War I Tale) (2014)

Hemingway appears in a single panel of Nathan Hale's engaging, hyper-researched account of World War I in digestible comic book form. Like in Art Spiegelman's *Maus,* the political sides are represented as animals, although Hemingway is human, along with Winston Churchill and J. R. R. Tolkien. (As mentioned elsewhere in this book, Hemingway was a volunteer ambulance driver in World War I.)

Hemingway in *Nathan Hale's Hazardous Tales,* 2014. © Abrams.

Tom the Dancing Bug (2014, 2012, 1999)

Ruben Bolling's "Computer Efficiency" strip is at once about Hemingway and not about Hemingway at all.

It's more about "technology, productivity, and creativity—and the fact that the very tool that authors, cartoonists, and really everyone uses to work is the exact same tool now that we use to distract ourselves in a million new and amazing ways," Bolling says.

To make his point, however, Hemingway was the perfect conduit.

"Hemingway is just a brand name," Bolling says. "I wanted to get him at the beginning of his career, so that his life would get sidetracked and he never would have his great legacy because of the technology right on his typewriter."

And shorthand, in comics, is essential.

"He is so iconic that if you say, 'This is Hemingway,' it's shorthand for an important American writer," Bolling says. "If I had chosen someone else, like Faulkner, I think it would have come with too much baggage. Is this comic about his writing style and how hard it is decipher? Or is it about Southern writers?"

Hemingway shows up twice more in *Tom the Dancing Bug,* as a part of Bolling's reductive-for-comedy's sake *Super-Fun-Pak Comix.* In 1999, Bolling tackled *The Old Man and the Sea.*

"It breaks the entire novel down into just a gag," Bolling says. "He works hard, thinks he has something great, and then he loses it—that is the structure of a three-panel gag. It's also the structure of this very important novel."

The Sun Also Rises in Tom the Dancing Bug's Super-Fun-Pak-Comix. © 2012 Ruben Bolling. Reprinted with permission of ANDREWS MCMEEL SYNDICATION. All rights reserved.

The Old Man and the Sea in Tom the Dancing Bug's Super-Fun-Pak-Comix. © 2019 Ruben Bolling. Reprinted with permission of ANDREWS MCMEEL SYNDICATION. All rights reserved.

Writer Fights (2014–2016)

Although R. E. Parrish studied linguistics in college, literature was always a passion—and that sensibility shows up in his internet comics. In one, he imagines a gritty reboot of a machete-wielding Mrs. Dalloway and in another, novelist Gabriel García Márquez opens a bar called "One Hundred Beers and Solid Tunes."

Here, it is Hemingway versus his feelings. Or F. Scott Fitzgerald.

It all started when Parrish was a grad student, drawing comics as a way to kill time between classes. "I think authors are a particular focus of mine just because there are so many biographical anecdotes that you can find about most authors that are just hilarious already, so it's not hard to cartoonize them," Parrish says.

All of Parrish's web comics can be read at reparrishcomics.com.

Courtesy R. E. Parrish.

Hemingway's first draft of *The Old Man and the Sea.* Courtesy R. L. Parrish.

The Life After (2014) and *Exodus: The Life After* (2016)

When office worker Jude wakes up to discover that his sterile, repetitive life actually is purgatory, he teams up with Hemingway to rebel against the celestial system.

According to creator Joshua Hale Fialkov, Hemingway was a relatively late addition to his series.

"The afterlife for suicides is the most mediocre day of your life, lived out ad infinitum. So, who committed suicide but never lived a truly mediocre day? We landed on Hemingway," says Fialkov.

In the book, Hemingway is Jude's sidekick, the shotgun-wielding heavy who also manages to have a ménage à trois with a pair of sexy demonesses—in what is strangely one of the more tender episodes in the book.

"Part of the fun is that so much of his bravado and swagger was clearly exaggerated," says Fialkov. "When you read his rough draft notes in any of his novels, the confident, ass-kicking man's man is usually missing. That degree of insecurity that's just bubbling under the surface is what makes him human, and a great foil for our protagonist."

This was the second time artist Gabo (aka Gabriel Bautista) depicted Hemingway; the first was in the gleefully blasphemous *Jesus Christ: In the Name of the Gun* (see pp. 94–101, this volume). In *Exodus,* the second series of *The Life After,* Gabo altered the design of Hemingway to reflect changes in the character.

"In *Exodus,* we find that the main character, Jude, is no longer leading the pack, and it now falls on Ernest to sort of pick up the pieces," says Gabo. "I decided it would be fitting to give him an outfit that was a tad more tactical by giving him a turtleneck sweater and some padded elbows and knees for combat. Later on in the *Exodus* series, we had to change his outfit once more to reflect his surroundings, and I felt a nice colorful Miami beach–inspired shirt would fit him well."

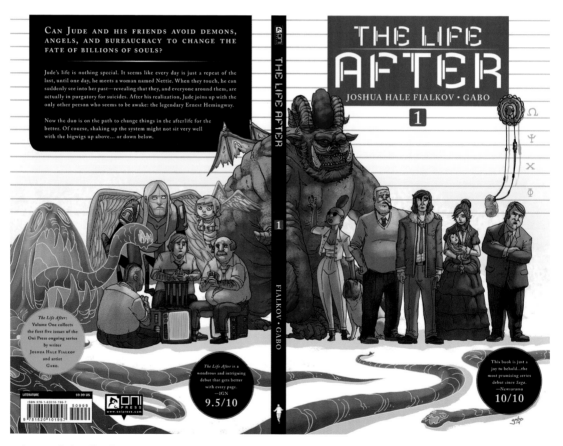

Volume 1 of *The Life After* cover.

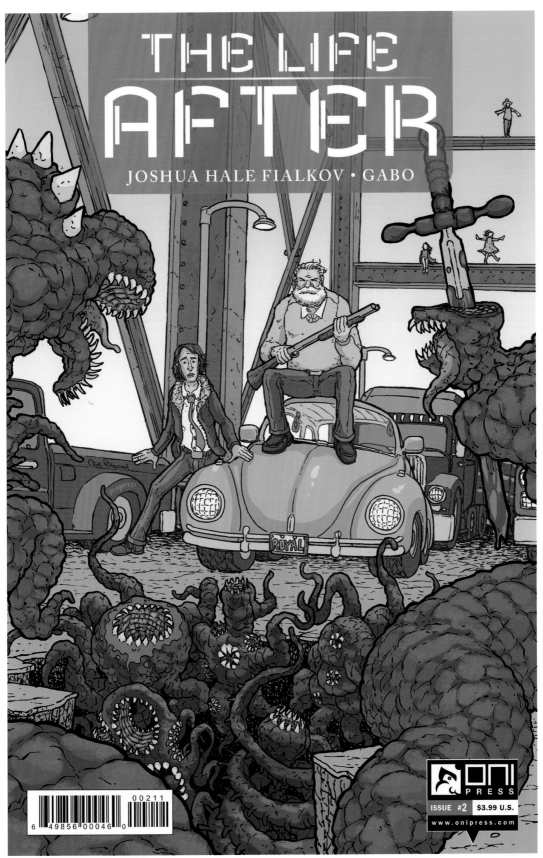

Cover of *The Life After* #2, with art by Nick Pitarra. From *The Life After* by Joshua Hale Fialkov and Gabo, published by Oni Press.

Page 71 from *The Life After* trade paperback, Vol. 2, in which Hemingway encounters Zelda and F. Scott Fitzgerald in the afterlife. From *The Life After* by Joshua Hale Fialkov and Gabo, published by Oni Press.

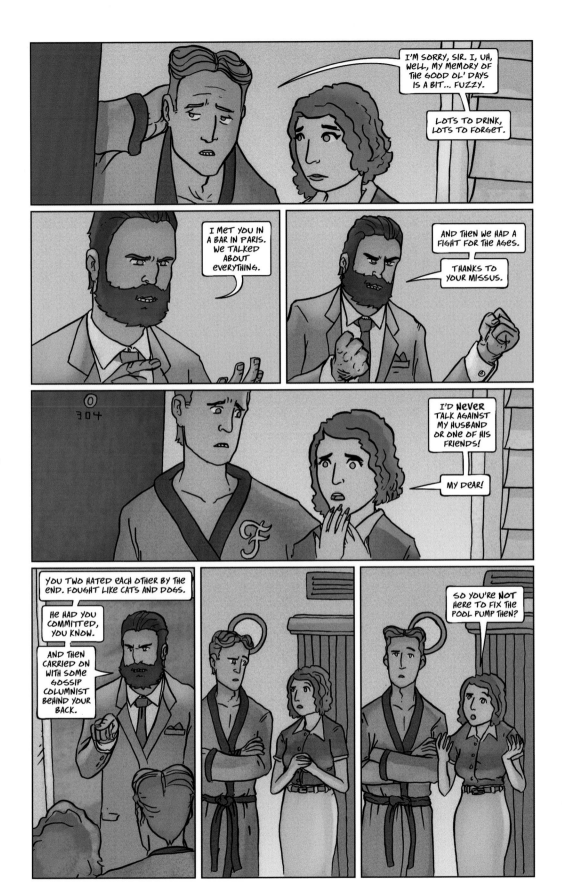

Page 72 from *The Life After* trade paperback, Vol. 2, in which Hemingway encounters Zelda and F. Scott Fitzgerald in the afterlife. From *The Life After* by Joshua Hale Fialkov and Gabo, published by Oni Press.

Page 77 from *The Life After* trade paperback, Vol. 2, which features Hemingway in Hell. From *The Life After* by Joshua Hale Fialkov and Gabo, published by Oni Press.

Page 78 from *The Life After* trade paperback, Vol. 2, which features Hemingway in Hell. From *The Life After* by Joshua Hale Fialkov and Gabo, published by Oni Press.

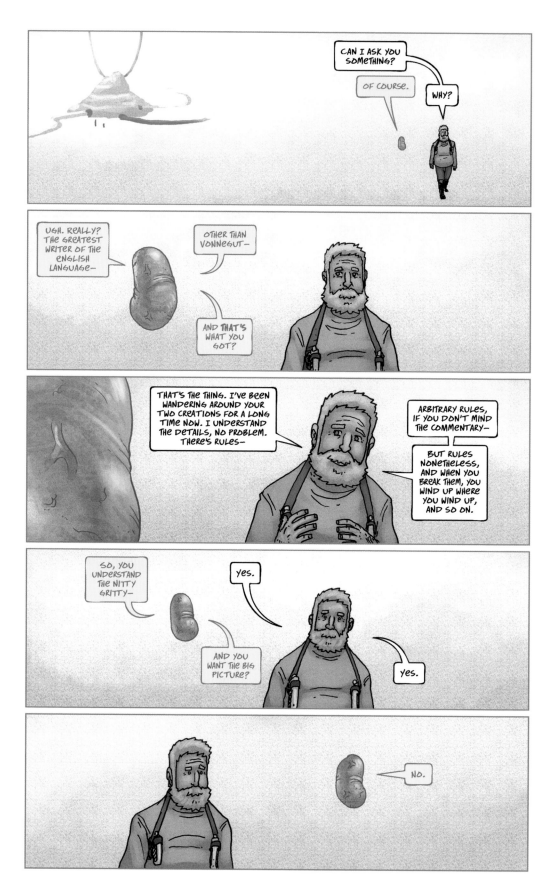

Page 64 from *The Life After* trade paperback, Vol. 3, in which Hemingway talks to God (who, in this reality, appears as a potato). From *The Life After* by Joshua Hale Fialkov and Gabo, published by Oni Press.

Page 65 from *The Life After* trade paperback, Vol. 3, in which Hemingway talks to God (who, in this reality, appears as a potato). From *The Life After* by Joshua Hale Fialkov and Gabo, published by Oni Press.

Cover of *Exodus: The Life After* #8 featuring Hemingway beating the tar out of a Mickey Mouse–like character in a park similar to Disney World. From *The Life After* by Joshua Hale Fialkov and Gabo, published by Oni Press.

老人と海 *"The Old Man and the Sea"* (2014)

This graphic novel adaptation by Rokuda Noboru was released as an e-book by eBookJapan. Rokuda, a prolific manga artist, made his professional debut in 1978 with *Saigo Test,* for which he was awarded the Shogakukan New Artist Award. He is best known for his sports manga series *Dash Kappei* (1980), which was adapted for television in 1981–82.

The Old Man and the Sea (2014)

Barcelona-based Miguel Montaner drew this as a self-promotional poster for his website, after rereading the novel.

"Hemingway's narrative style is very appealing and visual from the point of view of a graphic artist," Montaner says. "I've always been captivated by *The Old Man and the Sea.* This book is more accessible than other classics (for example, *Crime and Punishment*). So more people have read it and understand the references."

Cover for 老人と海 *"The Old Man and the Sea."*

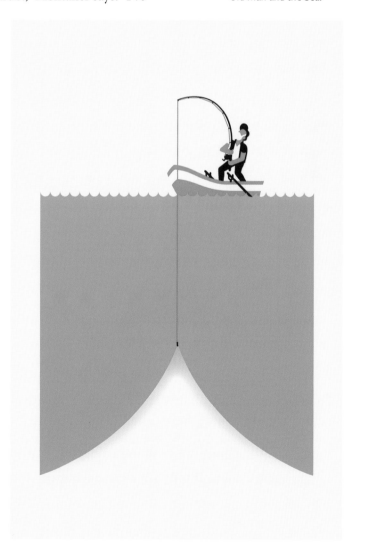

Poster for *The Old Man and the Sea.* By Miguel Montaner.

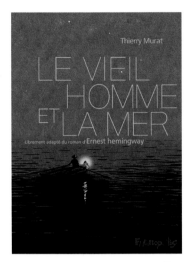

Cover of Thierry Murat's French-language graphic novel of *The Old Man and the Sea.*

Le Vieil Homme et La Mer (*The Old Man and the Sea*) (2014)

Thierry Murat's French-language graphic novel of *The Old Man and the Sea* features Hemingway as a stand-in for the audience. In an oceanside café, he hears a small boy's tale about his friend, the old fisherman who struggled to bring in a great marlin.

In the epilogue, Hemingway tells the boy that his story is beautiful. In response, the boy says, "C'est pas une histoire, m'sieur Hemingway. C'est la vie." ("This is not a story, Mr. Hemingway. It's life.")

Hemingway then goes home and writes the first line of the story.

I conducted a new interview with Murat, who kindly allowed his adaptation to be excerpted in this book (see pp. 181–184). Here, I've edited out my questions and let Murat tell the story of his adaptation, with the help of translator Plume Beuchat.

Thierry Murat on *Le Vieil Homme et La Mer* (*The Old Man and the Sea*)

I was about to turn 50, a time when we start to feel like we're getting old. There was the desire to adapt a great text from American literature into a comic book. A classic.

All at once, I remembered this very short, very strong book, *The Old Man and the Sea,* which relates in human terms what victory in defeat is.

This is what I had to speak about at this moment of my life.

So I relistened to Neil Young sing, "Old man look at my life, I'm a lot like you were . . ." in the song "Old Man" from his 1972 *Harvest* album. And then I spoke about it to my editor at Futuropolis.

We obtained the rights from the Hemingway family and there was a lot of rewriting to be done.

In the novel *The Old Man and the Sea,* at the start, the narrator is an omniscient, exterior narrator. And in my adaptation, the narrator is the child, Manolin, Santiago's apprentice. Hemingway is not in the original novel, but he's in my book. I decided to make the emblematic figure of the writer appear, like in Alfred Hitchcock's cameos in his own films, as a tribute.

Because of that, a justification was needed. So I decided to make the child tell the story of this old fisherman, who in turn tells it to Hemingway. And the reader concludes that it is thanks to this anecdote that my Hemingway character, at the end of my comic book adaptation, will have the idea to write his famous novel. This version, which is just pure fiction, of course, engages only myself and probably would have upset Hemingway [laughs].

He would have hated that we minimized the talent of an author by finding an outside source of inspiration for him. He liked to say that in his work all was invention, creation, and pure imagination. Which is totally false, of course. All authors who are not megalomaniacs will tell you that [laughs].

Telling this story from another point of view allowed me to completely appropriate the tale into a free adaptation. It was fresh outlook to try to suggest a personal reading. It's hard to tell the story of a man alone at sea with captions alone.

I don't know Hemingway's work, nor his life, very well. I am, above all, a fan of *The Old Man and the Sea.* But I really like his approach to literature.

Thierry Murat's sketchbook for his
adaptation of *The Old Man and the Sea.*

I like the way he brings us directly from point A
to point B, without circumvolution. His action is
sufficiently short to strike the reader, so the story
will stay in our memory forever. The form of his
writing is virile. And in its foundation, it can have a
feminine depth. The near-perfect balance?

It was my father who made me read *The Old
Man and the Sea* when I was 10 years old. I took a
lot of trips at sea with my father. The boat, the sail,
the ocean were all familiar during my childhood.
And later, as an adolescent, I read *A Moveable
Feast.* Those are the books that have the strong
scent of memory. The ones we don't forget.

To draw the old fisherman's boat, I asked my
father to make me a wooden model of the little
Cuban boat. It is 40 centimeters long and it sat

on my worktable when I was drawing *The Old
Man and the Sea.* I could turn it around, look
at its profile, from above, in the light, or in the
shade. And this boat became, little by little by
looking at it, a true character. It's what I wanted.
For it to be alive. I like live objects. Otherwise I
don't know how to draw them.

We all want, like Corto Maltese, to meet a
character like Hemingway, to sit at a table, facing him, and to ask him how to get by in life, how
to deal with this damn existence which we don't
always know what is for. And we would all like to
hear him answer: "Go to hell, kid, with your stupid
questions! Read my books and buy me another
mojito!"

Thierry Murat uses this
model boat for his drawings.

*The Old Man and the
Sea.* By Thierry Murat. ©
Futuropolis. 2014. Used
with permission.

On dirait qu'il va beaucoup moins vite...

Tu commences à en avoir ta claque, poisson !

De temps en temps, il sortait sa main de l'eau salée pour l'exposer au soleil.
Dès qu'elle était sèche, il la replongeait à nouveau.

Mois aussi, poisson. Je commence
à trouver le temps long.

By Thierry Murat. © Futuropolis.
2014. Used with permission.

By Thierry Murat. © Futuropolis.
2014. Used with permission.

Grendel vs. The Shadow #1 (2014)

What Matt Wagner's parents passed away, one of the few things he kept from their house was a vintage typewriter that'd been stashed away in the attic.

"I took it to a guy here in Portland who restores old typewriters, and he told me it was the same model as Hemingway's favorite," says Wagner, the artist and writer behind the *Grendel* series. "Once I'd decided that Hunter Rose would have a private collection of artifacts from both famous writers and flamboyant criminals, the typewriter was one of the first things I drew on the page."

An assassin and crime lord, Grendel is the masked alter ego of author and rich socialite Hunter Rose. In this series, Rose accidentally travels back in time to 1930s New York, where he encounters the Shadow (the pulp hero

This and facing page: Hemingway's typewriter in *Grendel,* 2019. © Matt Wagner. Used with permission.

whom Orson Welles once voiced on the radio). Hemingway's typewriter also appears in other comics in this collection, notably in *The Life After* (pp. 174–175) and *Superman / Wonder Woman* (p. 188).

"Human actions have historical resonance, and these objects serve as a reminder of those whose lives affected society in ways both good and bad, long after the actors are gone," Wagner says. "It seemed obvious that Hunter Rose, with his grand sense of drama and arrogance, would retain such a collection . . . relics of those famous personas whose stars burned (nearly) as bright as his own."

Other relics in the antihero's collection include Aldous Huxley's eyeglasses, Ned Kelly's armored helmet, and the newly acquired ashes of the villainous Shiwan Khan, which sets the story of *Grendel vs. The Shadow* in motion.

Hemingway is discussed in *kuš!* Courtesy Roman Muradov. "Priest Picnic. *kuš!* comics."

kuš! #22 (2015)

Hemingway shows up, although indirectly, in Roman Muradov's work in the "Fashion" issue of *kuš!* an international comics art anthology published in Latvia. Muradov also illustrated Hemingway in Image Comics' *Glory* in 2012 (see p. 128, this volume).

"It is actually a sort of tribute to Hemingway, although through a slightly twisted perspective," Muradov says.

The story is also reprinted in *Aujourd'hui, Demain, Hier,* a collection of Muradov's work from Dargaud.

Superman / Wonder Woman #13 (2015)

Ponder this: in DC Comics' New 52 Universe, Superman uses Hemingway's typewriter, a birthday gift from Bruce Wayne, aka Batman. When Wonder Woman teases him for using such an "ancient relic," Superman explains, "Sometimes the sound of the keys hitting the paper helps me compose my thoughts better."

"I can type fast, but I can't write fast," he says.

"I liked the idea of Batman / Bruce Wayne giving his friend Superman / Clark Kent a Hemingway typewriter due, of course, to Clark's secret identity being a kick-ass reporter," says writer Peter Tomasi. "I imagined it was the typewriter that Hemingway wrote his Spanish Civil War dispatches on—a period in history I had a deep interest in it due to a relative who served in the Lincoln Brigade."

Superman owns Hemingway's typewriter in *Superman / Wonder Woman #13,* January 2015. © DC Comics.

Carver #1–5 (2015–2016)

Chris Hunt's hard-boiled, two-fisted hero looks and dresses like Hemingway in the 1920s—and that's no accident. Part homage to Hugo Pratt's *Corto Maltese* series (see pp. 17–18, this volume), part mash-up of Hemingway and Indiana Jones, Carver is a way for Hunt to deconstruct male archetypes.

"I believed there was some truth to the archetype in some way, and I wanted to find a way to introduce something that was recognizable," says Hunt, who wrote and illustrated the five-issue, creator-owned series for Z2 Comics.

Hunt is a native of Idaho; he says the "specter of Hemingway paints over things here." This spirit makes it into his work, where artist-turned-soldier-turned-adventurer Francis Carver tries to unravel a kidnapping plot in 1923's Paris.

If you look closely, you can find F. Scott Fitzgerald talking to a sailor whom Hunt refers to as his "Bootleg Corto Maltese." Paul Pope, Hunt's friend and mentor, also provides some backup stories and covers for the series.

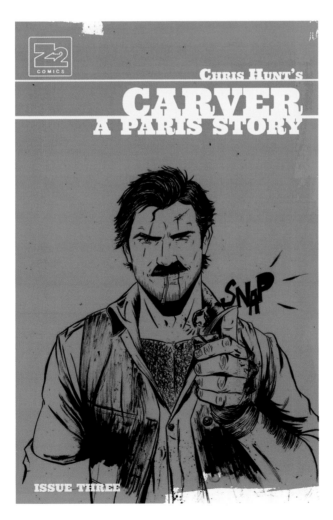

The hero in Chris Hunt's Carver has Hemingway's looks. *Carver* by Chris Hunt.

Page 8 of *Carver* #1. Art and story by Chris Hunt. Used with permission of Chris Hunt.

Page 9 of *Carver* #1. Art and story by Chris Hunt. Used with permission of Chris Hunt.

Page 10 of *Carver* #1. Art and story by Chris
Hunt. Used with permission of Chris Hunt.

Page 11 of *Carver* #1. Art and story by Chris Hunt. Used with permission of Chris Hunt.

Page 12 of *Carver* #1. Art and story by Chris Hunt. Used with permission of Chris Hunt.

Page 27 of *Carver* #1, which shows a short vignette illustrated by Paul Pope with the story by Chris Hunt. Used with permission of Chris Hunt.

Page 28 of *Carver* #1, which shows a short vignette illustrated by Paul
Pope with the story by Chris Hunt. Used with permission of Chris Hunt.

Page 29 of *Carver* #1, which shows a short vignette illustrated by Paul Pope with the story by Chris Hunt. Used with permission of Chris Hunt.

James Joyce: Portrait of a Dubliner (2016)

The winner of Spain' s National Comic Prize, Alfonso Zapico's *James Joyce: Portrait of a Dubliner* celebrates the life and legend of the Irish author. Hemingway shows up in a few panels to support Joyce and his magnum opus, *Ulysses.*

Hemingway's quotation in the book is taken from a 1922 letter he wrote to Sherwood Anderson: "Joyce has a most goddamn wonderful book. It'll probably reach you in time. Meantime the report is that he and all his family are starving but you can find the whole celtic crew of them every night in Michaud's where Binney and I can only afford to go about once a week. . . . The damned Irish, they have to moan about something or other but you never heard of an Irishman starving."

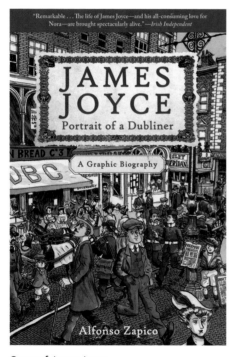

Cover of *James Joyce: Portrait of a Dubliner* and one of its panels featuring Hemingway.

谷崎万華鏡—谷崎潤一郎マンガアンソロジ (*Tanizaki Kaleidoscope: A Tanizaki Jun'ichiro Manga Anthology*) (2016).

Published by Chuo Koron Shinsha, this collection of graphic novel adaptations of Tanizaki Jun'ichiro's works commemorates the fiftieth anniversary of this famous novelist's death. One story in this Japanese collection, by Shiriagari Kotobuki, is a remix of Hemingway's *The Old Man and the Sea* with Tanizaki's *Diary of a Mad Old Man* (1961).

Tanizaki's story is about a 77-year-old man who, despite recovering from a stroke, cannot tame his raging libido and finds himself lusting after his daughter-in-law as his body decays. Upon reading the story, Shiriagari was shocked by this depiction of a lecherous old man trying to wring the last drop out of his life and remembered Hemingway's tale. Finding the situation analogous to Santiago's obsession with the marlin at the end of his life, he decided to intertwine the two stories into one graphic vision. He offers his sincere apologies to Tanizaki and Hemingway fans alike.

Cover of *Tanizaki Kaleidoscope,* which includes a Hemingway-inspired story.

Rough Riders Nation #1 (2016)

In Adam Glass's *Rough Riders* series, Theodore Roosevelt recruits boxer Jack Johnson, sharpshooter Annie Oakley, magician Harry Houdini, and others to battle an alien threat. At the turn of the twentieth century, Hemingway would have been in short pants—but he'll show up in future stories, says creator Glass.

Rough Riders Nation #1, published by Aftershock, lays out the mythology of the teams that gather in each decade, and Hemingway joins in the 1930s. But he might appear in the series before then, says Glass: "There's a story that takes place in World War I, and let's just say a young Hemingway will appear."

Best known as a writer and producer for TV shows like *Supernatural* and *Criminal Minds,* Glass has also found time to write comics like *Suicide Squad* and *Luke Cage Noir.* His love for Hemingway endures, and he looks forward to using Papa more in future installments of *Rough Riders.*

"There'll never be another Hemingway. There can't be," Glass says. "There's a lot of gray there, which is what makes him so great. He's not as black and white as the pages he wrote on."

Hemingway will make an appearance in *Rough Riders Nation.* Art by Alberto Ponticelli. Courtesy AfterShock Comics, LLC, 2016. Used by permission.

The Newsboy Legion: Boy Commandos Special #1 (2017)

The Golden Age–era *Newsboy Legion* was Howard Chaykin's first exposure to Jack Kirby's work, so when the chance came to revisit these obscure World War II characters, he jumped at it.

The story is about the Boy Commandos— namesakes of another Kirby title, created with Joe Simon—coming to New York to interact with the Newsboy Legion. Hemingway serves as the Jimmy Olsen of the story, giving the boys their marching orders to foil a Nazi plot.

Chaykin first read Hemingway's *Death in the Afternoon* in Spanish class and hated it. He has since become more of an admirer, though one with a critical eye.

"When I look at Hemingway's portrayal of a hero, it remains two-dimensional in that lack of self-awareness," Chaykin says. "I always felt that Fitzgerald and Hemingway together would have made the perfect writer . . . they would have been able to create convincing heroes with feet of clay, without sacrificing the heroic nature of the character."

Hemingway in *The Newsboy Legion: Boy Commandos.*

"Literary Love Triangle: The Making of Hemingway's *The Sun Also Rises*" (2017)

Nathan Gelgud (*A House in the Jungle*) was creating weekly comics for the Signature Reads website when Mary V. Dearborn's *Ernest Hemingway: A Biography* was released. It proved to be the perfect news hook to revisit the genesis of *The Sun Also Rises*.

"I was rereading some Sammy Harkham comics at the time, and I think you can see it in the piece," Gelgud says. "The way I put 'Paris 1926' at the top is taken from the way he opened his story 'The New Yorker Story,' which is a great literary comic."

Gelgud used photo references for the piece, but he admits that for Hemingway, "if you just can draw a kind of burly guy and give him the right hair and mustache, you're almost all the way there. But I did use that one of him at the typewriter, and there's a photo of the gang in Paris that's directly referenced in the comic. That kind of direct reference is appealing in comics, like redrawing a book cover or doing a drawing of a painting."

Gelgud shared his connection with his father, who admired Hemingway's short story "The Three-Day Blow" (1925). In the story, Nick Adams and his friend Bill get drunk and talk about baseball, the St. Louis Cardinals, and Nick's recent heartbreak.

"Twenty years ago my dad told me about that story and said, 'He really nailed it,'" Gelgud remembers. "I think about that a lot, that idea of 'nailing it'—just getting the tone of something so right that a reader can say, 'Yup, that's it.' I'd like to do something about working in a restaurant that nails it. Or about first moving to New York."

Ernest Hemingway with friends at a café, Pamplona, Spain. Ernest Hemingway (*left*), Harold Loeb (wearing glasses), Lady Duff Twydsen (wearing hat), Elizabeth Hadley Richardson, Donald Ogden Stewart, Pat Guthrie. Ernest Hemingway Collection. John F. Kennedy Presidential Library and Museum, Boston.

ERNEST HEMINGWAY WAS ON FORCED HIATUS FROM THE TWO WOMEN HE LOVED, WHILE HE WAITED FOR HIS FIRST NOVEL TO BE RELEASED.

— Pauline, if this isn't cleared up by Christmas I'm going to KILL MYSELF

JUST THE PREVIOUS YEAR, HE CLAIMED HE HAD NO INTEREST IN WRITING A NOVEL.

THE NOVEL IS AN AWFULLY ARTIFICIAL AND WORKED OUT FORM.

AROUND THE SAME TIME, HE TOOK A TRIP TO SPAIN WITH HIS WIFE HADLEY AND SOME OF THEIR FRIENDS.

HE STARTED WRITING UP AN EMBELLISHED ACCOUNT OF THE TRIP.

OH, YOU'RE WRITING A NOVEL?

ONLY BECAUSE I'M SICK OF HEARING EVERYONE TALK ABOUT *THEIR* NOVELS

HADLEY WOULD READ HIS PAGES EVERY NIGHT...

YOU MIGHT CONSIDER NOT USING REAL NAMES?

"Literary Love Triangle: The Making of Hemingway's *The Sun Also Rises.*" July 2017. © Nathan Gelgud. Reprinted with permission of the artist. All rights reserved.

...A WEIRD ROLE FOR HER, AS SHE WAS THE ONLY ONE FROM THE GROUP WHO WAS LEFT OUT OF THE STORY.

WHILE HE WAS WRITING HIS NOVEL, HIS DEBUT STORY COLLECTION WAS RELEASED, AND GOT GOOD REVIEWS.

HIS MOTHER CHOSE TO SEND HIM A REVIEW THAT CITED STRONG INFLUENCE FROM GERTRUDE STEIN AND SHERWOOD ANDERSON, WHICH SURELY RANKLED HIM.

F. SCOTT FITZGERALD LOVED HIS FRIEND'S NOVEL, *THE SUN ALSO RISES*, AND ACTED AS HEMINGWAY'S AGENT FOR IT.

JOLLY GOOD SHOW, OLD BOY...

...THOUGH I DARE SAY, YOU OUGHT TO CUT THE FIRST TWENTY PAGES.

THAT WINTER, THE HEMINGWAYS VACATIONED IN SCHRUNS, AUSTRIA...

...WHERE THEY WERE JOINED FOR A BIT BY THEIR NEW FRIEND PAULINE PFEIFFER.

LATER, HEMINGWAY LEFT FOR NEW YORK, WHERE HE SIGNED A CONTRACT WITH SCRIBNER'S FOR *THE SUN ALSO RISES.*

"Literary Love Triangle: The Making of Hemingway's *The Sun Also Rises*." July 2017. © Nathan Gelgud. Reprinted with permission of the artist. All rights reserved.

FROM THERE, HEMINGWAY WENT TO PARIS.

THAT'S WHERE PAULINE WAS.

WHEN HADLEY FOUND OUT ABOUT ERNEST AND PAULINE'S ONGOING AFFAIR, SHE AT FIRST TRIED TO TOLERATE IT.

THE THREE OF THEM EVEN COHABITED IN SPAIN.

BUT EVENTUALLY, HADLEY DEMANDED THAT HER HUSBAND NOT SEE PAULINE FOR 100 DAYS. AFTER THAT, THEY COULD DECIDE WHAT THEY WANTED TO DO.

I'M GOING MAD

SO HEMINGWAY WAITED OUT THE SEPARATION IN PARIS.

AFTER A WHILE, HADLEY RELENTED, ALLOWING ERNEST AND PAULINE TO BE REUNITED.

YOU'RE NOT MY PROBLEM ANYMORE.

THE SUN ALSO RISES WAS RELEASED TO RAVE REVIEWS.

THE SUN ALSO RISES

ERNEST HEMINGWAY

AND HEMINGWAY'S MOM WAS SURE TO SEND HIM A CLIPPING FROM THE CHICAGO TRIBUNE.

ERNEST HEMINGWAY CAN BE A DISTINGUISHED WRITER IF HE WISHES TO BE. HE IS, EVEN IN THIS BOOK, BUT IT IS A DISTINCTION HIDDEN UNDER A BUSHEL OF SENSATIONALISM AND TRIVIALITY. "

"Literary Love Triangle: The Making of Hemingway's *The Sun Also Rises*." July 2017. © Nathan Gelgud. Reprinted with permission of the artist. All rights reserved.

HEMINGWAY ☜ BURROUGHS ☜ GEVINSON ☜   ROBINET ☜ BERG ☜ WARE ☜ SIMIC ☜

Hemingway in *Answer Book,* 2017. © Marc Stopeck.

Answer Book (2017)

In Oak Park, Illinois's weekly *Wednesday Journal*'s *Answer Book,* Marc Stopeck illustrates Hemingway along with other literary heroes who called Oak Park home, among them Edgar Rice Burroughs, Tavi Gevinson, and cartoonist Chris Ware, who also drew a young Hemingway (see pp. 115–116, this volume).

"Hemingway: A Lonely Life" (2017)

Gavin Aung Than drew this piece for his book *Creative Struggle: Illustrated Advice from Masters of Creativity* (2018) and published it on his website, ZenPencils.com. He used Hemingway's Nobel Prize acceptance speech as the basis for the narrative.

"I was focusing on illustrating quotes specifically about art and creativity," recalls Aung Than. "I knew Hemingway was a keen fisherman so I thought it would be fun to have his struggle catching a marlin as a metaphor for trying to catch writing inspiration."

As an Australian, Aung Than didn't read Hemingway's book in school.

"I only read *The Old Man and the Sea* but knew about his exciting life," Aung Than says. "He had an almost superhero myth about himself—the fighter, drinker, soldier, raconteur—he was larger than life. He also had an iconic look, which all makes for a great comic character!"

HEMINGWAY
A Lonely Life

...WITH GREAT LUCK...

...HE WILL SUCCEED.
- ERNEST HEMINGWAY

EXCERPT FROM THE NOBEL PRIZE SPEECH "ERNEST HEMINGWAY - BANQUET SPEECH". NOBELPRIZE.ORG. © NOBEL MEDIA AB 2017

zen pencils.com

Doomsday Clock #2 (2017)

When DC merged its comic book universe with Alan Moore's *Watchmen*, the characters knew something was wrong, just not *what*.

When Adrian Veidt (aka Ozymandias) and street sleuth Rorschach conduct some research at the Gotham City Public Library, they spot three busts above the doorway: Ernest Hemingway, Virginia Woolf, and Vladimir Mayakovsky.

Rorschach comments that the three authors "had something in common." Their shared thread? Suicide.

Doomsday Clock is written by Geoff Johns and penciled by Gary Frank.

Hemingway's bust in
Doomsday Clock #2.

Double 7 (2018)

In this work, scripted by Yann and drawn by artist André Juillard and set during the Spanish Civil War, Hemingway and his mistress / future wife Martha Gellhorn are bit players in a story of war-torn love and intrigue between a spirited Spanish freedom fighter and a Russian pilot.

Early in the story, when Hemingway introduces Gellhorn as "My girl-friend Martha," she's quick to correct him. "Martha Gellhorn. And not 'girlfriend.' 'Special correspondent' for *Collier's,* an American magazine!"

Hemingway and Martha Gellhorn in *Double 7.* © Yann and André Juillard. Published by Dargaud.

Ernest Hemingway with Ilya Ehrenburg and Gustav Regler during the Spanish Civil War. Ernest Hemingway Collection. John F. Kennedy Presidential Library and Museum, Boston.

Above: Hemingway is one of four novelists in *Writer Fighters.* Courtesy Stephen Conn.

Facing page: An exchange between Hemingway and Fitzgerald that echoes real life in *Writer Fighters.* Courtesy Stephen Conn.

Writer Fighters (2018)

In Stephen Conn's *Writer Fighters,* set in 1937, four booze-fueled novelists band together to fight the Fascist Spanish dictator Francisco Franco. The US government recruits a superteam of writers with otherworldly powers: Ernest Hemingway, F. Scott Fitzgerald, William Faulkner, and James Joyce. Hemingway, when drunk, turns into a shirt-shredding, Hulk-like monster who smashes things for the greater good.

Conn describes the graphic novel, which he self-published in 2018, as a "five-plus year labor of love." The spark for the story, he says, was Mathew J. Bruccoli's 1994 book *Fitzgerald and Hemingway: A Dangerous Friendship.*

"I became fascinated by the yin and yang of their relationship—Hemingway the protégée who gradually becomes the master as Fitzgerald's fortunes wane," Conn remembers.

He first attempted the idea as an animated trailer while attending New York City's School of Visual Arts (the 2008 demo, *20th Century Masters,* can still be seen on YouTube, at https://www.youtube.com/watch?v=OAIOO2RzmAM). He then wrote it as a feature-length screenplay, before crafting the current graphic novel incarnation. Conn is currently searching for an indie publisher for the project.

On this page, Hemingway and Fitzgerald sort through their fraught history, in an exchange that echoes a letter Fitzgerald sent Hemingway in July 1936. That summer, Hemingway had published "The Snows of Kilimanjaro" in *Esquire* with the passage:

"He remembered poor Scott Fitzgerald and his romantic awe of them and how he had started a story once that began, 'The rich are different from you and me.' And how some one had said to Scott, Yes, they have more money. But that was not humorous to Scott. He thought they were a special glamorous race and when he found they weren't it wrecked him as much as any other thing that wrecked him."

Fitzgerald, correctly, thought this was Hemingway kicking him when he was down, and he wrote: "Please lay off me in print. . . . If I choose to write *de profundis* sometimes it doesn't mean I want friends (still friends, then?) praying aloud over my corpse. . . . And when you incorporate it (the story) in a book would you mind (gently, gently) cutting my name?"

To Hemingway's credit and that of his editor, Max Perkins, Fitzgerald's name was struck from collected versions. Then, however, Fitzgerald suffered the indignity of dying before Hemingway and again had his manhood questioned in Hemingway's memoir *A Moveable Feast.*

De Hemingway Triatlon (*The Hemingway Triathlon*, 2018)

Dirk-Jan Hoek posted pages of his Hemingway opus *De Hemingway Triatlon* online before he found a publisher, Sherpa, in the Netherlands.

Set in 1956, the story finds Hemingway struggling to overcome writer's block and impotence after winning the Nobel Prize for Literature.

But the project didn't start out with Hemingway.

"The idea was to write a story about macho men," says Hoek. He thought of Hemingway, although he didn't know much about the author. But in reading Hemingway's novels and short stories, Hoek became interested in not only Hemingway's work but also his life.

"In the first drafts, he had a small part, but he moved himself to the front of the stage, as you would expect from him," Hoek remembers. "For me, he became much more interesting when I found out that he built his own legend, for the most part. He is so much like a comic book character—at least his image is. My book tries to show another side of him."

Hoek's story is fiction, including the Hemingway Triathlon itself, in which the author replaced the regular sporting activities with "hunting, fucking, and drinking."

"But true or not true, my story does paint a real picture of the author and his obsession with his macho image, an image that became harder to sustain when he grew old and his body and mind paid the toll of drinking and war,

The cover for *The Hemingway Triathlon* (*left*) and creator Dirk-Jan Hoek (*right*).

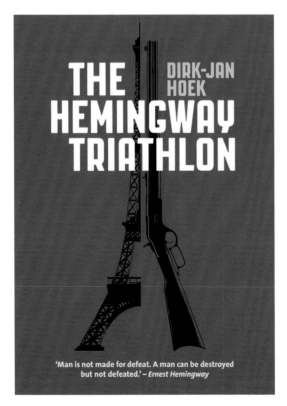

'Man is not made for defeat. A man can be destroyed but not defeated.' – *Ernest Hemingway*

The Hemingway Triathlon.
Courtesy Dirk-Jan Hoek. © 2018.
More information: www.sherpa.
nu or www.dirk-janhoek.com.

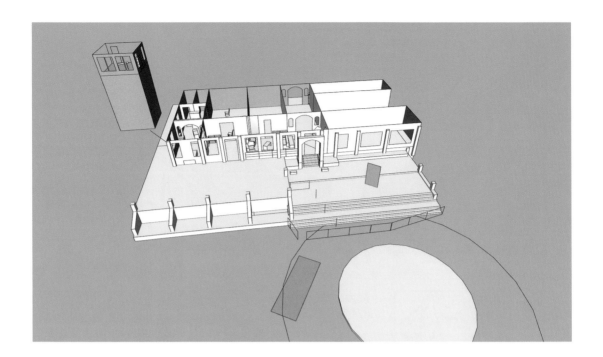

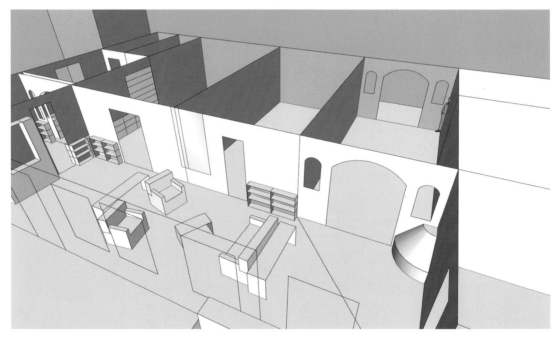

Views of the 3-D model of Hemingway's house for *The Hemingway Triathlon.*

car and plane crashes. What happens when the gap between image and reality becomes too wide?"

For Hoek, the answer is an easy one. "I think it makes a person very unhappy. The conclusion of the book is that you'd better learn to accept your shortcomings and not inflate yourself too much."

Hoek traveled to Cuba to take photos of Finca Vigía, Hemingway's home in Havana's San Francisco de Paula Ward.

"I measured the house with footsteps," Hoek says. "At home I built a 3-D model from it, to help me with the scenes in and around the house. It was fun, but I would not do it again. A lot of work. I loved his house—it was beautiful, very tasteful."

Hoek had read Mary Hemingway's *How It Was,* which helped him learn more about the home. "They had their own carpenter in Cuba who made their furniture. She wrote about a magazine display she had designed and had a carpenter build. I recognized it in the house; I love those kind of details."

For more information on Hoek and his work, see www.sherpa.nu or www.dirk-janhoek.com.

This and following pages: The Hemingway Triathlon. Courtesy Dirk-Jan Hoek, © 2018. More information: www.sherpa.nu or www.dirk-janhoek.com.

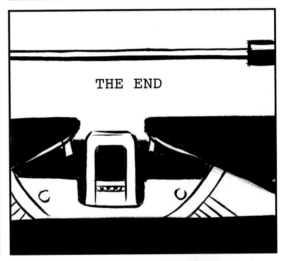

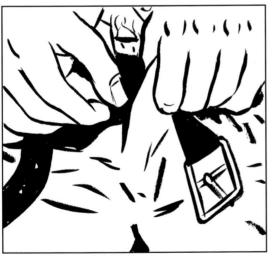

NO ERNEST,
IT WON'T COME BACK...

...I MUST BE HONEST WITH YOU: IF IT'S BEEN LONGER THAN 12 MONTHS, IT WON'T COME BACK.

BE REALISTIC... WITH YOUR DRINKING... AND THAT CRASH WOULDN'T HAVE DONE YOU ANY GOOD.

HOW'S YOUR HEAD?

WHY DON'T YOU JUST ACCEPT IT? YOU'VE GOT THREE CHILDREN.

THERE ARE OTHER WAYS TO PLEASE MARY.

IT'LL COME BACK!

AND DON'T SAY ANYTHING TO MARY!

ERNEST
HEMINGWAY
1954

ALFR
NOBEL

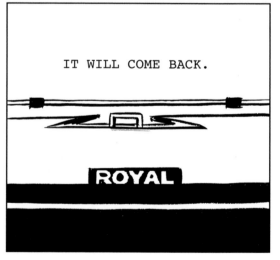

IT WILL COME BACK.

2020–

Hemingway Comics
and the Future

"Hemingway: Hell or High Water" (work in progress)

It was a match made on the internet. Or Reddit, at least.

Croatian artist Miljenko Šimić was looking for a graphic novel to illustrate. American novelists Anthony Mathenia (*Paradise Earth: Day Zero*) and Shane Crash (*Forest Life)* wanted to break into comics and were sitting on a script titled "Hemingway: Hell or High Water," a tale of the author hunting Nazi submarines off the coast of Florida during World War II.

"I was amused by the humorous, almost irreverent style of it," Šimić says. "The script didn't shy away from dealing with the author's brooding soul, and I started appreciating it even more."

For Mathenia, it was a perfect match. "We all share a love for Hemingway. That's the magic."

This graphic novel was in production as *Hemingway in Comics* was being written, discovered by Chris Hunt (*Carver*) on Instagram, where Šimić was sharing images of his work. "Drawing comics is a fun but demanding task requiring constant problem-solving," Šimić says. "You want to do justice to such an important figure [as Hemingway]."

As for the story, Mathenia and Crash consulted various reference works, such as Terry Mort's *The Hemingway Patrols: Ernest Hemingway and His Hunt for U-Boats* (2009).

There has been some debate about whether Hemingway was actually hunting for U-boats. Famously, Hemingway's third wife, Martha Gellhorn, said the patrols were "nothing more than a fancy excuse to get gas rations."

Mathenia and Crash's story chooses the more dramatic scenario.

"We wondered how it would have played out if he had actually faced
a U-boat armed with only grenades and tommy guns on his sport fishing
yacht, *Pilar,*" Mathenia says. "The comic was originally conceived as an
action-oriented piece of alternative history, pitting the author against a
Kriegsmarine crew."

When Šimić joined the creative team, however, "it gave us an opportunity to dig deeper and further develop the story and characters. While
we are playing fast and loose with the official history, historical accuracy
remained a major consideration," says Mathenia.

In Mathenia and Crash's story, Hemingway's adversary is a young German submarine officer named Heinrich, "who is trying to survive long
enough to get back to his lover," says Mathenia. "Our aging Hemingway
is a victim of his own celebrity; a past-his-prime matador trying to relive
past glory in the arena of war."

The confrontation off the Florida coast forces both men to "come to terms
with what it means to be a man in the face of adversity," says Mathenia.

"Our main goal is to be true to the spirit of Hemingway's life and writing. The story is thematically inspired by books like *A Farewell to Arms*
and *The Sun Also Rises,*" Mathenia says. "There are also nods and Easter
eggs to his other works sprinkled throughout the book."

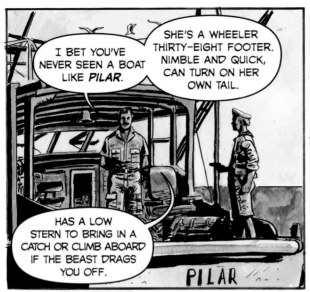

I BET YOU'VE NEVER SEEN A BOAT LIKE *PILAR*.

SHE'S A WHEELER THIRTY-EIGHT FOOTER. NIMBLE AND QUICK, CAN TURN ON HER OWN TAIL.

HAS A LOW STERN TO BRING IN A CATCH OR CLIMB ABOARD IF THE BEAST DRAGS YOU OFF.

PILAR

I HAD THE FLYING BRIDGE INSTALLED TO GET A BETTER VIEW OF THE HUNT. IT'S MARVELOUS ON A CLEAR DAY.

CAN YOU EXPLAIN *ZE* ANTENNA?

WITH THE WAR, IT'S AN EPIC POEM TO GET A TANK OF DIESEL.

SO I TRACK MARLIN MIGRATION FOR THE ACADEMY OF NATURAL SCIENCES.

AND THEY KEEP MY TANK FILLED IN MANY WAYS.

I WARNED YOU, OLD MAN, *NO TRICKS!*

"Laguna Hemingway" (work in progress)

In "Laguna Hemingway," Italian author and artist Luca Pozza tackles a period of Ernest Hemingway's life seldom seen in comics. Notably: Hemingway's struggle in 1948 to finish his novel *Across the River and into the Trees*.

Pozza's comic book, in production when *Hemingway in Comics* went to print, finds the author duck hunting in a lagoon near Venice, Italy—only to be caught in a strange dream that leads him to confront his father's suicide and talk with figures from his past and present, notably his ex-wives, his muse Adriana Ivancich, Orson Welles, Ezra Pound, Marlene Dietrich, and Errol Flynn, among others.

Pozza says "Laguna Hemingway" was inspired by his desire to explore Hemingway's "relationship with the Veneto region" and "show the dark side of the writer, the shadow of death that accompanied him all his life."

Pozza's comic book mirrors both Hemingway's life and the story of Col. Richard Cantwell, the lead character in Hemingway's 1950 *Across the River and into the Trees*. In the novel, Cantwell remembers his life and lost loves in the last days of his life.

"In this story, 'my' Hemingway is already descending the parabola that is leading him to depression," Pozza says. "The conversations with the people in his life represent the self-analysis of a man who is no longer a braggart at the top of his game, but instead a tired man in his twilight years who begins to feel the approach of death."

Particularly potent in Pozza's watercolor panels is Hemingway's tortured relationship with his father and his guilt over his father's suicide.

"His father represents Death in person," Pozza says. "Frightened, Hemingway shoots Death, and it is only then that he discovers that in reality behind the mask is the father. Maybe Hemingway kills his father in a Freudian sense."

But there is a sense of reconciliation.

"Hemingway apologizes for the shooting and his father minimizes the incident, saying that it's not worth spoiling the day. But Hemingway opens his heart. . . . He apologizes for having accused him of ruining the family. In short, the whole matter of his father's suicide is told between the lines," Pozza says.

Pozza thinks Hemingway's life continues to be fertile ground for comic book creators because "he really had an exceptional life . . . he certainly lived outside the rules. . . . We could write hundreds of books on the various aspects of his life, but I chose the comics, because it's the storytelling medium that I prefer, and because it allows you to trespass into the fantastic without difficulty."

An opening page from Luca Pozza's "Laguna Hemingway," which depicts the suicide of Hemingway's father, Dr. Clarence Edmonds "Ed" Hemingway, who will show up later in the narrative.

Here, we jump to page 51 from Luca Pozza's "Laguna Hemingway," in which the author encounters Death, who also happens to be a relative.

Page 52 from Luca Pozza's "Laguna Hemingway,"
in which Hemingway encounters Death, who also
happens to be a relative.

Page 53 from Luca Pozza's "Laguna Hemingway," in which Hemingway encounters Death, who also happens to be a relative.

Page 54 from Luca Pozza's "Laguna Hemingway," in which
Hemingway encounters Death, who also happens to be a relative.

Page 55 from Luca Pozza's "Laguna Hemingway," in which Hemingway encounters Death, who also happens to be a relative.

Page 56 from Luca Pozza's "Laguna Hemingway," in which Hemingway
encounters Death, who also happens to be a relative.

These frames, of page 24 from Luca Pozza's "Laguna Hemingway," feature another Hemingway run-in with figures from his past, the gender-swapping Zelda and F. Scott Fitzgerald.

Hemingway Oddities and Ephemera

Even when the author is not directly featured, the name Hemingway pops up in magazines and other comics. An "E. Hemingway" is listed as a contributor to *Cracked* #130 (January 1976), although there's no corresponding story. Other references are less opaque.

National Lampoon (April 1, 1979)

Hemingway isn't lampooned, oddly, in the 1979 April Fool's issue of *National Lampoon.* Instead, he appears in caricature form for the magazine's "Lives of the Great" feature.

Among the true facts in the illustration: "In 1944, a jealous Hemingway destroyed the portrait of his lover with a submachine gun. A stray shot blew apart her toilet and flooded the apartment."

Yama-Yama (1981)

Hemingway appears in name only, credited as the coauthor (with "Hans Cristian Andersen"), of a story that appears in Robert Williams's underground comic *Yama-Yama,* a flip-book collaboration with S. Clay Wilson. In *Hysteria in Remission: The Comix and Drawings of Robt. Williams,* editor Eric Reynolds writes that the raw, pornographic comic was meant to "mock a proliferation of punk rock comics. . . . Crude and vulgar were the aims."

Williams would gain mainstream attention later in the 1980s for his infamous cover for Guns N' Roses' first major label record, *Appetite for Destruction,* also the title of his cover painting. After an uproar from retailers, Williams's painting was moved to the interior of the album in favor of the skulls and crucifix cover by Billy White Jr.

Hemingway is credited in *Yama-Yama. The Ugly Head,* December 1981. © Robert Williams and S. Clay Wilson.

Jon Sable, Freelance #19 (1983)

Olympic athlete–turned-mercenary Jon Sable finds himself being hunted by those responsible for his family's death. The series combines several of his personal loves: geography, Tarzan, big game hunting, and Hemingway.

Close to the western summit there is the dried and frozen carcass of a leopard.

No one has explained what the leopard was seeking at that altitude."

–Ernest Hemingway
THE SNOWS OF KILIMANJARO

Hemingway's influence is clear in *Jon Sable, Freelance* #19.

Puma Blues #3 (1986)

Edward Khanna—who read the original *Comics Journal* articles that provide the seedlings for this book—pointed out a Hemingway reference in the beginning of *Puma Blues,* written by Stephen Murphy and illustrated in mind-boggling detail by Michael Zulli.

"A character, Jack, has a beard at the time and looks Hemingway-esque and is describing a nightmare he had to his class, which includes a scene with Death holding up a phone and saying 'It's for you,' which I assume is a reference to *For Whom the Bell Tolls,*" wrote Khanna.

"Rereading the part, I noticed that in the sequence just prior to it, there's a robot named 'Ernest,' who leaves his master to go find himself in nature."

Hemingway-esque character in *Puma Blues.*

HBO's "Loved to Death," *Tales from the Crypt,* season 3 (1991)

Strictly speaking, this isn't a comic book, but it is also too weird not to include. Expanding the definition of *Hemingway in Comics,* this cover features the author's granddaughter, actress Mariel Hemingway.

HBO's *Tales from the Crypt* cable TV series (1989–96) sought to capture the gory morality tales of William Gaines's original comic book of the same name (1950–55). In this episode, "Loved to Death," a struggling screenwriter played by Andrew McCarthy finds himself getting too much of a good thing when a love potion works too well on his neighbor, an aspiring actress played by Hemingway.

Each episode of the anthology was introduced by the decaying, pun-obsessed Crypt Keeper and featured a comic book cover that echoed the style of Gaines's original series. This cover, drawn by Mike Vosburg, appeared in color as the episode began.

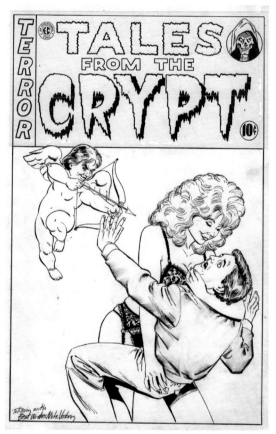

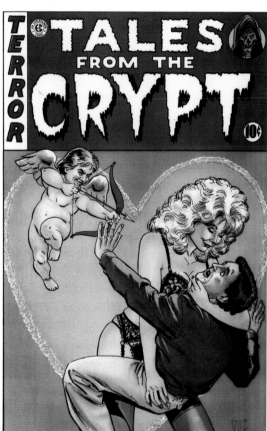

As part of his image research process, Vosburg would come to set and take reference photos. Here, we can see Mariel Hemingway with and without her blond wig, from a fantasy sequence.

This was not Mariel's first brush with comics, however. In 1987, she starred as Lacy Warfield in *Superman IV: The Quest for Peace,* replacing Lois Lane as the blue Boy Scout's love interest and damsel in distress. In the comic book

Top, left and right: Mike Vosburg's original photos featuring Mariel Hemingway from HBO's *Tales from the Crypt* episode.

Above: Tales from the Crypt comic book that was turned into a TV episode with the help of Hemingway's granddaughter.

Mariel Hemingway inspired the comic book adaptation of *Superman: The Quest for Peace.*

adaptation of the movie, however, almost none of the characters resemble their on-screen counterparts—though you can judge for yourself whether Ms. Hemingway made an impact on the illustrators.

Druid (1995)

Doctor Druid's cab driver and sidekick in Warren Ellis's 1995 comic book series is named Hemingway. He's not treated very well.

Generation X #5 (1995)

Comics writer-editor Danny Fingeroth directed us to *Generation X* for a villain named Hemingway. As part of supervillain team Gene Nation, the hulking, spiny Hemingway terrorized both humans and mutants, making appearances across several X-Men–related series, until he ran afoul of Wolverine in 2004's *Weapon X* #21 (volume 2). He was first drawn by Chris Bachalo in 1995.

Trilogia—O homem Que Não se Chamava Hemingway (The Man Who Wasn't Called Hemingway) (1995)

Portugese writer-artist Victor Mesquita's trippy meditation on art and identity features talking sharks, shark/gun hybrids, and, of course, Hemingway himself.

Hombres y Héroes (2004)

Hombres y Héroes (published by Mexico's Novedades Editores) gave Hemingway the full biographical treatment. And strangely, like stories in *Vidas Ilustres* and *WildC.A.T.s Covert Action Teams,* the artists made him a blond.

EN ESTE APACIBLE LUGAR, *HEMINGWAY* PASARÍA EL TIEMPO PESCANDO, LEYENDO Y ESCRIBIENDO. ENVIABA INFATIGABLEMENTE SUS TRABAJOS LITERARIOS A REVISTAS GRANDES Y PEQUEÑAS, LAS CUALES SE LOS DEVOLVÍAN CON LA MISMA REGULARIDAD.

A blond Hemingway in *Hombres y Héroes.*

Brave and the Bold #24 (2007, third series)

Milestone Comics' teen hero Static fights crime by night, but by day as Virgil Hawkins, he attends Ernest Hemingway High School.

"I'm not sure who on the creative team actually named the school Ernest Hemingway High," recalls artist John Paul Leon. "I distinctly remember drawing the first establishing shot of the school around page 10 of issue 1."

Leon says it's likely that cocreator Dwayne McDuffie or writer Robert Washington III named the high school, though Leon can't swear to it. McDuffie died in 2011 and Washington in 2012. Via Twitter, Static cocreator Michael Davis (@mdworld) related that he wasn't sure who the Hemingway fan was: "I think it was Dwayne [McDuffie.] BUT it may have been [writer Christopher] Priest."

Deathstroke, vol. 2, #8 (2012)

In DC Comics' New 52 line, the name of Deathstroke's nurse is Hemingway—possibly a reference to Hemingway's romance with nurse Agnes von Kurowsky during World War I. She patches up the warrior assassin over some playful chitchat.

Wednesday Journal editorial comic (2013)

When a martial arts gym was proposed for the Hemingway District along Oak Park Avenue in Hemingway's hometown, there was a mild uproar among the existing businesses. Marc Stopeck, editorial cartoonist for the *Wednesday Journal*, imagines how Hemingway might have weighed in. Flying V Martial Arts now calls Oak Park Avenue home.

Hemingway in a *Wednesday Journal* editorial comic.

Hemingway Comic Roundup

Not every comic requires commentary, so here are a few in their native habitat: comics surrounded by other comics.

Rose Is Rose—Thursday, February 15, 1996

Arlo and Janis—Thursday, March 22, 2001

Arlo and Janis—Friday, March 23, 2001

Original illustration done by Walter Molino to document the
death of Ernest Hemingway, which took place on July 2, 1961,
likely published in the Italian magazine *Domenica del Corriere*.
This painting may have been done when Hemingway's death
was still being reported as an accident.

Baldo—Tuesday, September 5, 2017

Frank & Ernest—October 17, 2003

"YOU'RE LUCKY TO HAVE YOUR CASE TRIED BY JUDGE HEMINGWAY. HE'S KNOWN FOR HIS SHORT SNAPPY SENTENCES."

AFTER A ROUGH DAY OF RUNNING WITH THE BULLS, ERNIE, SCOTT, ZELDA, GERTIE AND ALICE DECIDED ON A RELAXING THREE HOUR CRUISE...

"WHICH WINE GOES BEST WITH 'THE OLD MAN AND THE SEA'?"

Dan Panosian

"Has anyone ever told you your tweets are Hemingwayesque?"

"Just when I was feeling good about myself, she called me a visual cliché."

OCTOBER 28, 1954: ERNEST HEMINGWAY IS AWARDED THE NOBEL PRIZE IN LITERATURE "DEMONSTRATED IN THE OLD MAN AND THE SEA." UNABLE TO ATTEND THE CEREMONY DUE TO INJURIES FROM A PLANE CRASH, HEMINGWAY CELEBRATES BY IMAGINING HIMSELF WRESTLING HIS FELLOW PRIZE WINNERS, THE SWEDISH ROYALTY, AND ALL OF STOCKHOLME.

AT ONCE.

Chuck Dillon

An illustration of Hemingway by Argentinian artist Ricardo Heredia, done specifically for this book in 2019.

Acknowledgments

This book wouldn't have been possible without the Kent State University Press's acquiring editor, Will Underwood, and director, Susan Wadsworth-Booth, who both thought this whole idea was just weird enough to work. They were right, and this is the most fun I've had working on any book.

Editor Mary Young helped organize the manuscript into a compelling, readable form; designer Christine Brooks made it beautiful; and copy editor Erin Holman made the prose stronger and lither. Darryl Crosby created the most amazing book catalog of my career, and Richard Fugini has been a publicity sage.

Before I ever pitched this idea as a book, editor Dan Nadel of the *Comics Journal* commissioned a series of (long) pieces about Hemingway in comics, and the Ernest Hemingway Foundation of Oak Park asked me to present the material at the International Hemingway Conference in 2016. It's all snowballed from there. John Sutton at Sheridan College asked me come out to Wyoming to for an art gallery showing of the work I'd collected and a lecture, and Jace Gatzemeyer asked me to speak at the American Literature Association's annual conference in Boston. So, it's all your fault. Thanks for your belief in the strangest project to ever get a book contract.

Craig Yoe and Eric Reynolds offered guidance and advice at the beginning of the project, and I'm grateful to all you all. Also, the staff at Fantagraphics—including Jacquelene Cohen, RJ Casey, Nancy Clarke, and Paul Baresh—were incredibly patient and helpful.

Raegan Carmona at Andrews McMeel helped me track down cartoonists and rights and was amazing throughout a long process. Julie Grahame at the Estate of Yousuf Karsh not only helped me with photo rights but also assisted with fact-checking (what color was that sweater again?) and citations.

Special thanks to archivist Sarah Breaux and curator Benjamin Clark at the Charles M. Schulz Museum and Research Center in Santa Rosa, California, who helped me with all things Sparky.

Thanks to Klaus Strzyz, who helped me track down the very first comic in this project, *Der Ausflug nach Key West* (*The Trip to Key West*) from Germany's *Adventures of Uncle Scrooge Treasury* #3 (1984). I can't thank you enough, my friend, for your time and kindness through the years.

Melissa Arroyo, Katherine Foley, and Susan McKean served as my archivists, researchers, assistants, and moral support through the project. Elan Richardson-Omamo helped build the first version of our website, HemingwayinComics.com, and then Lejla Subasic stepped in to polish it up and help edit the book's index.

So many friends, fellow scholars, and readers of the *Comics Journal* suggested entries and helped with translation, and I'm indebted to you all. Thanks to John Wells for helping identify the *Weird War* and *Superman* stories and providing scans. Rich Donnelly and Steve Donnelly of Cool Lines Artwork (coollinesartwork.com) were invaluable in helping me track down a high-resolution scan of Mike Vosburg's *Tales from the Crypt* cover featuring Mariel Hemingway from HBO's TV series. Ger Apeldoorn directed me to the *Coogy* comic strips, and then he (with the aforementioned Craig Yoe) led me to "The Old Man and the Sea" in *Frantic* #1, which was also featured in *Behaving Madly,* Apeldoorn and Yoe's excellent book about *Mad* magazine imitators. Nat Gertler suggested the inclusion of *Heavy Hitters,* Chris Hunt pointed me to "Hemingway: Hell or High Water," and Phil Rippke helped me find *Samurai Crusader.*

Plume Beuchat, Gaëlle Ramet, and Caroline S. Stauffer provided invaluable translation help. Special thanks to Mark Cirino for his translation assistance and to Gianluigi Filippelli for his very helpful blog post on *Topolino*'s 8 X 8 . . . 49 project. At the eleventh hour, my old friend Hoyt Long came to the rescue with vital translations for Hemingway comics in Japanese. Thanks again, my good man. Aaron Vetch provided professional copyediting and caught some heart-stopping mistakes, for which I owe him a drink. Or many.

Folks like Ryan Holmberg, Greta Crippa, Sean Michael Robinson, Sandeep Atwal, and so many more offered their time, passion, and expertise, and I thank you all.

Thanks to the continued support of my friends here in Oak Park, particularly Leigh Tarullo, Emily Reiher, and Debby Preiser at the Oak Park Public Library. John Berry, Barbara Ballinger, and Keith Strom at the Ernest Hemingway Foundation of Oak Park continue to be friends and supporters. Special thanks to Frank Lipo, Rachel Berlinski, and Elizabeth Nichols at the Historical Society of Oak Park and River Forest for helping me with scans and research.

I had such great collaborators on this project, and contributor Jace Gatzemeyer would like to express his deep gratitude for the support of the Hemingway Society and the Lewis-Reynolds-Smith Founder's Fellowship in producing his piece.

This book would not have been possible without the generous contributions and permissions from scores of authors, artists, editors, and publishers. Thanks to each of you for sharing your love (or complicated love-hate) of Hemingway with a wider audience.

And finally, my wife, Betsy, has put up with my curiosities and eccentricities for a lot of years. She's my Superwoman, cape or not. Thanks, my dear.

Bibliography and
Further Reading

Note: Not all comics and cartoons listed here are referenced in this book, but we hope that this noncomprehensive list will lead to future scholarship.

Adams, Scott. *Dilbert,* July 7, 1997. https://licensing.andrewsmcmeel.com/features/dt?date=1997-07-07.

Acharya, Satish. "Old Men of Indian Politics!" *World of an Indian Cartoonist,* May 14, 2011. http://cartoonistsatish.blogspot.com/2011/05/old-men-of-indian-politics.html?m=1.

Alajalov, Constantin. *Ernest Hemingway. Vanity Fair,* Mar. 1934. Available online at the Smithsonian Institution Libraries website, http://www.sil.si.edu/exhibitions/Celeb/gallery05.htm.

Aldrich, Lance, author, and Gary Wise, illustrator. *Real Life Adventures.* Apr. 13, 2012. https://licensing.andrewsmcmeel.com/features/rl?date=2012-04-13.

———. *Real Life Adventures.* May 7, 2010. https://licensing.andrewsmcmeel.com/features/rl?date=2010-05-07.

Amend, Bill. *Foxtrot,* May 21, 2003. https://licensing.andrewsmcmeel.com/features/ft?date=2003-05-21.

Armstrong, Robb. *Jumpstart,* July 4, 2001. https://licensing.andrewsmcmeel.com/features/jt?date=2001-07-04.

Bagley, Aaron. *Educational Poster #36: Alcoholic Authors,* 2013. *A. Bagley* (blog), http://aaronbagley.blogspot.com/.

Baron, Mike, author, and Mike A. Nelson, artist. "A Movable Beast." *Heavy Hitters Annual* #1. New York: Marvel Comics, 1993.

Bates, James, author, and John Costanza, artist. "The Bald Man in the Sea." *Simpsons Comics* #135. Santa Monica, CA: Bongo, 2007.

Beeler, Nate. *The Old Mitt and the Sea,* Mar. 7, 2012. https://www.cagle.com/nate-beeler/2012/03/primary-problem.

Binder, Otto, author, and C. C. Beck, artist. "The Glory of Tomorrow." *Captain Marvel Adventures* #110. *New York:* Fawcett Publications, July 1950.

Block, Herbert. *The Old Man of the Sea,* drawing. May 1942. Available online at the Library of Congress website, http://www.loc.gov/pictures/item/2010635752/.

Bocquet, Jose-Luis, author, and Catel Muller, artist. *Kiki de Montparnasse.* New York: Abrams, 2012.

Bolling, Ruben. "Computer Efficiency: Ernest Hemingway's New Typewriter." *Tom the Dancing Bug,* Oct. 31, 2014. https://licensing.andrewsmcmeel.com /features/td?date=2014-10-31.

————. "Tom the Dancing Bug's Super-Fun-Pak Comix." *Tom the Dancing Bug,* Jan. 6, 2012. https://licensing.andrewsmcmeel.com/featurestd?date= 2012-01-06.

————. "Tom the Dancing Bug's Super-Fun-Pak Comix." *Tom the Dancing Bug,* Oct. 16, 1999. https://licensing.andrewsmcmeel.com/features/td?date= 1999-10-16.

Cannon, Zander. "The Death of Ernest Hemingway." *Murder Can Be Fun* #2. San Jose: Slave Labor Graphics, 1996.

Cantu, Hector, author, and Carlos Castellanos, artist. *Baldo,* Sept. 5, 2017. https://licensing.andrewsmcmeel.com/features/ba?date=2017-09-05.

Castelli, Alfredo, author; Gordon Bass, author; Michael Regnier, author; Grazia Nidasio, author; Guglielmo Milani, author; Hugo Pratt, author; Rene Goscinny, author, et al. "La Juve su due Fronti: Europa Italia." *Corriere de Ragazzi* #197239. Milan: Corriere Della Sera, Sept. 1972.

Catalano, Joe, author; George Gladir, author; E[rnest] Hemingway, author; John Severin, artist; Bill Ward, artist; Don Orehek, artist; Charles Rodrigues, artist; et al. "Dyn-O-Mite." *Cracked* #130, Jan. 1976.

Chast, Roz. *A Computer Program That Helps You Write a Novel. New Yorker,* May 27, 1996.

————. *Poet in Hiding. New Yorker,* May 28, 2001.

Chaykin, Howard. "A Separate Peace in Pieces!" *The Newsboy Legion; Boy Commandos Special* #1. Burbank, CA: DC Comics, Aug. 2017.

Choi, Brandon, author; Jonathan Peterson, author; Mat Broome, artist; Troy Hubbs, artist; Sal Regla, artist; and Al Vey, artist. "Endangered Species, Part 1: For Whom the Bells Toll / Recruitment." *WildC.A.T.s Covert Action Teams* #41. Portland, OR: Image Comics, Aug. 1992.

Choi, Brandon, author; Jonathan Peterson, author; Mat Broome, artist; and Sean Parsons, artist. "Endangered Species, Part 2: Brothers in Arms" *WildC.A.T.s Covert Action Teams* #42. Portland, OR: Image Comics, Sept. 1992.

Conn, Stephen. *Writer Fighters.* Self-published, 2018.

Constantin, Sunnerberg. *Writers.* Feb. 12, 2018. www.Cartoonstock.com.

Corriveau, Jeff. *DeFlocked,* Feb. 8, 2016. https://licensing.andrewsmcmeel.com /features/dft?date=2016-02-08.

Crash, Shane, author; Anthony Mathenia, author; and Miljenko Šimić, artist. Hemingway: Hell or High Water." Work in progress.

Dedini, Eldon. *While He Was in Paris, Warren Knew Picasso, Miro, Hemingway, Stravinsky, Cocteau, and Fitzgerald. Nothing Ever Came of It. New Yorker.* Mar. 29, 1993.

Dudak, Fort. *Fort Dudak's Six Pack* #3. Seattle, WA: Apostate Mansion Press, 2009.

Duffy, J. C. *"Ask Not for Whom the Bell Tolls?" I Don't Believe I Did, Actually,* Aug. 23, 2016. www.Cartoonstock.com.

Dunn, Alan. *"It's the Only Book That Brings You the Real Paris—the Paris of Leonard Merrick and Ernest Hemingway." New Yorker.* Mar. 9, 1935.

Dunham, Chip. *Overboard,* Nov. 12, 2016. https://licensing.andrewsmcmeel .com/features/ob?date=2016-11-12.

———. *Overboard,* July 11, 2017. https://licensing.andrewsmcmeel.com/features/ob?date=2017-07-11.

Duval, Yves, author, and Edouard Aidans, artist. "Dan Cooper Revient." *Tintin* #568. Brussels: Les Editions du Lombard, Jan. 1960.

———. *Les meilleurs recits de Aidans et Duval* #8. Brussels: Loup, 2003.

Ellison, Harlan, author, and Eric Shanower, artist. *Harlan Ellison's Dream Corridor* #2. Milwaukie, OR: Dark Horse, Mar. 2007.

Ellis, Warren, author, and Leonardo Manco, artist. *Druid* #1–4. New York: Marvel Comics, 1995.

Estrada, Ric. "Mercy Brigade." *Our Army at War* #234. New York: DC Comics, July 1971.

———. "The Old Man and the She." *Frantic!* #1 N.p.: Pierce Publishing, Oct. 1958.

Evans, Greg. *Luann,* Feb. 3, 1988. https://licensing.andrewsmcmeel.com/features/lu?date=1988-02-03.

Fialkov, Joshua Hale, author, and Gabriel Bautista, artist. *The Life After.* Portland, OR: Oni Press, 2014.

———. *Exodus: The Life After* #1–2. Portland, OR: Oni Press, 2015.

———. *Exodus: The Life After* #3–10. Portland, OR: Oni Press, Inc, 2016.

Forcelloni, Marco. "Il papero che volle farsi re" (The Duck Who Wanted to Make Himself King). *Topolino* #2341. Modena: Mondadori, Disney Italia, Panini Comics, 2000.

Freccero, Andrea. "Zio Paperone e l'equivoco scottante" (Uncle Scrooge and the Big Misunderstanding). *Topolino* #2353. Modena: Mondadori, Disney Italia, Panini Comics. 2001.

Fry, Michael, author, and T Lewis, artist. *Over the Hedge,* May 14, 1997. https://licensing.andrewsmcmeel.com/features/oh?date=1997-05-14.

———. *Over the Hedge,* May 1, 2018. https://licensing.andrewsmcmeel.com/features/oh?date=2018-05-01.

Gauld, Tom. "What Did You Write Today, Mister Hemingway?" *You're All Just Jealous of My Jetpack.* Montreal: Drawn & Quarterly, May 2012.

Geary, Rick. *Blanche Goes to Paris.* Seattle, WA: Headless Shakespeare Press. 2001.

Gelgud, Nathan. "Literary Love Triangle: The Making of Hemingway's The Sun Also Rises." July 2017, www.signature-reads.com. Site discontinued as of Nov. 26, 2019.

Glass, Adam. *Rough Riders Nation* #1. Sherman Oaks, CA: AfterShock Comics, 2016.

Grant, Allen. "Death Trek 100, Part Two: Analysis of a Story Where the Writer Runs Out of Plot." *Lobo,* vol. 2, #36. New York: DC Comics. 1997.

Gronle, Thomas; Titus Ackermann, and Jonas Greulich. *100 Meisterwerke der Weltliteratur.* Berlin: Egmont Comic Collection, Sept. 2009.

Hagen, Ralph. *The Old Man and the Noodle,* Nov. 27, 2005. www.Cartoonstock.com.

Hale, Nathan. "11/11 at 11:00." *Nathan Hale's Hazardous Tales: Treaties, Trenches, Mud, and Blood (A World War I Tale).* New York. Abrams, 2014.

Hall, Jason, author, and Cliff Chiang, artist. "Act I." *Beware the Creeper* #1. New York: DC Comics, June 2003.

———. "Act II." *Beware the Creeper* #2. New York: DC Comics, July 2003

———. "Act V." *Beware the Creeper* #5. New York: DC Comics, Aug. 2003.

Hama, Larry, author, and Marc Silvestri, artist. "Blood, Sand, and Claws!" *Wolverine* #35. New York: Marvel Comics, Jan. 1991.

———. " . . . It Tolls for Thee." *Wolverine* #36. New York: Marvel Comics, Feb. 1991.

———. "Fall Back and Spring Forward." *Wolverine* #37. New York: Marvel Comics, Mar. 1991.

Harrell, Rob. *Adam@Home,* Nov. 10, 2018. https://licensing.andrewsmcmeel .com/features/ad?date=2018-11-10.

Harris, Sidney. *Can You Believe How Many Students Can't Identify Socrates, Hemingway and Churchill?* Oct. 17, 2006, www.Cartoonstock.com.

———. *Hemingway's Dog Meets Faulkner's Dog,* Oct. 10, 2006. www.Cartoon stock.com

———. *Influences,* Oct. 17, 2006. www.Cartoonstock.com.

Hayes, Nick. *Poetry in Practice: Ernest Hemingway: For Naomi Wood and Her New Novel, Mrs. Hemingway.* Naomi Wood's website, Feb. 4, 2014. https:// naomiwood.com/category/mrs-hemingway/page/5/.

Hemingway, Edward, and Mark Bailey. *Hemingway & Bailey's Bartending Guide to Great American Writers.* Chapel Hill: Algonquin, 2007.

Hemingway, Ernest, and Gavin Aung Than. *Hemingway: A Lonely Life. Zen Pencils,* June 26, 2017. https://zenpencils.com/comic/hemingway.

Higgins, Kyle, author, and Eduardo Pansica, artist. "Circle of Life." *Deathstroke,* vol. 2, #8. New York: DC Comics, June 2012.

Hoek, Dirk-Jan. *Der Hemingway Triatlon (The Hemingway Triathlon).* Haar-lem, Netherlands: Sherpa, 2018.

Hunt, Chris. *Carver* #1. New York: Z2 Comics, 2015.

———. Carver #2–5. New York: Z2 Comics, 2016.

Inzana, Ryan. "Hemingway." Work in progress.

———. *Ichiro.* Boston: Houghton Mifflin / Houghton Mifflin Harcourt, 2012.

Jason [John Arne Sæterøy]. *The Left Bank Gang.* Seattle, WA: Fantagraphics, 2006.

———. "Papa." *Pocket Full of Rain and Other Stories.* Seattle, WA: Fanta-graphics, 2008

———. *Pop!* Oslo: Jippi, 2016. P1.

Johns, Geoff, et al. *Doomsday Clock.* New York: DC Comics, 2019.

Johnson, Jimmy. *Arlo and Janis,* Mar. 22, 2001. https://licensing.andrewsmc meel.com/features/aj?date=2001-03-22.

———. *Arlo and Janis,* Mar. 23, 2001. https://licensing.andrewsmcmeel.com /features/aj?date=2001-03-23.

Kabatek, Adolf. *"Der Ausflug nach Key West"* (The Trip to Key West). *Adventures of Uncle Scrooge Treasury* #3. Stuttgart: Ehapa Verlag, 1984

Keatinge, Joe, author, and Roman Muradov, artist. "Bloodshadow Part 2: Relent-less." *Glory.* Portland: Image Comics, Nov. 2012.

———. "Glory." Glory. Portland: Image Comics, Apr. 2012.

Kelley, Steve, author, and Jeff Parker, artist. *Dustin,* Sept. 10, 2011.

Kick, Russ, author, and Steve Rolston, artist. *The Graphic Canon.* Vol. 3, *From Heart of Darkness to Hemingway to Infinite Jest.* New York: Seven Stories Press, 2012.

Knight, Keith. *The Knight Life,* Jan. 28, 2016. https://licensing.andrewsmcmeel .com/features/kl?date=2016-01-28.

Konier, Irek. *Fisherman Story: En Attendant Hemingway.* Grenoble: Glénat Benelux, 2004.

Koren, Edward. *"Hemingway! Is He Any Good?"* New Yorker, Sept. 14, 1987.

Kupperberg, Paul, author, and Frank Miller, artist. "The Greatest Story Never Told." *Weird War Tales* #68. New York: DC Comics, 1978.

Kraft, David Anthony, author, and Klaus Janson, artist. "Part One: The Origin of Null and Void!" *World's Finest Comics* #304. New York: DC Comics, 1984.

Leiknes, Mark. *Cow and Boy Classics,* Sept. 14, 2008.

Lobdell, Scott, author, and Chris Bachalo, artist. "Big Time in the Big Apple." *Generation X* #5. New York: Marvel Comics, 1995.

Lo Porto, Tiziano, author, and Daniele Marotta, artist. *Superzelda: The Graphic Life of Zelda Fitzgerald.* New York: One Peace Books, 2012.

MacNelly, Jeff. *Ernest the Cat I.* Jeff MacNelly website, http://www.jeff-macnelly .com/ernest-1.htm.

MacNelly, Susie, author, and Gary Brookins, artist. *Shoe,* Aug. 26, 2012.

——. *Shoe,* July 31, 2014.

MacPherson, Duncan. *Ernest Hemingway,* 1981. McCord Museum, Montreal, Quebec. Available online at https://www.musee-mccord.qc.ca/en/collections /duncan-macpherson-fonds/.

Maggin, Elliot S! "The Biggest Game in Town!" *Superman* #277. New York: DC Comics, Apr. 1974.

Males, Marc, and Jean Dufaux. *Hemingway: Muerte de un Leopardo.* Grenoble: Glenat, 1993.

Mallett, Jef. *Frazz,* Oct. 30, 2002. https://licensing.andrewsmcmeel.com/features /fz?date=2002-10-30.

——. *Frazz,* Mar. 1, 2003. https://licensing.andrewsmcmeel.com/features/fz ?date=2003-03-01.

——. *Frazz,* Mar. 1, 2003. https://licensing.andrewsmcmeel.com/features/fz ?date=2003-03-01.

——. *Frazz,* Aug. 12, 2004. https://licensing.andrewsmcmeel.com/features/fz ?date=2004-08-12.

——. *Frazz,* Nov. 10, 2004. https://licensing.andrewsmcmeel.com/features /fz?date=2004-11-10.

——. *Frazz,* Jan. 18, 2007. https://licensing.andrewsmcmeel.com/features/fz ?date=2007-01-18.

——. *Frazz,* July 21, 2007. https://licensing.andrewsmcmeel.com/features/fz ?date=2007-07-21.

——. *Frazz,* Aug. 13, 2010. https://licensing.andrewsmcmeel.com/features/fz ?date=2010-08-13.

——. *Frazz,* Nov. 8, 2011. https://licensing.andrewsmcmeel.com/features/fz ?date=2011-11-08.

——. *Frazz,* Oct. 26, 2018. https://licensing.andrewsmcmeel.com/features/fz ?date=2018-10-26.

Marlette, Doug. "Whatcha Got There, Boy?" *Kudzu.* Sept. 13, 1981. Available online at the Library of Congress website, http:/www.loc.gov/pictures/item /2008677239/.

Maslin, Michael. *A Bialy, a Latte, and "A Farewell to Arms."* New Yorker, June 23, 1997.

Matena, Dick. *Sartre and Hemingway.* Zelhem, Netherlands: Arboris Verlag, 1992.

McDonnell, Patrick. *Mutts,* May 29, 2013. www.comicskingdom.com.

McPherson, John. "By Their Fourth Date, Debbie Started to Feel Like Steve Was Sort of a 'Momma's Boy.'" *Close to Home,* Oct. 25, 2010. https://licensing .andrewsmcmeel.com/features/cl?date=2009-07-24.

———. "A Farewell to Arms." *Close to Home,* July 30, 2018. https://licensing .andrewsmcmeel.com/features/cl?date=2018-07-30.

Meddick, Jim. *Monty,* May 21, 2015. https://licensing.andrewsmcmeel.com /features/mt?date=2015-05-21.

———. *Monty,* July 26, 2018. https://licensing.andrewsmcmeel.com/features /mt?date=2018-07-26.

———. *Monty,* Aug. 1, 2018. https://licensing.andrewsmcmeel.com/features /mt?date=2018-08-01.

———. *Monty,* Aug. 3, 2018. https://licensing.andrewsmcmeel.com/features /mt?date=2018-08-03.

Mesquita, Victor. *Trilogia—O homem Que Não se Chamava Hemingway* (The Man Who Wasn't Called Hemingway), 1995. http://victormesquita.com. Site discontinued as of Nov. 26, 2019.

Millar, Mark, author; John McCrea, artist; and James Hodgkins, artist. "There's Nothing I Haven't Sung About." *Jenny Sparks: The Secret History of the Authority* #5. New York: Wildstorm (DC), 2000.

Milligan, Peter, author, and Colleen Doran, artist. "A Portrait of the Metan . . ." *Shade, the Changing Man* #31. New York: DC Comics, 1993.

———. "Last Sacrament." *Shade, the Changing Man* #32. New York: DC Comics, 1993.

Molino, Walter. Untitled Hemingway death illustration. Milan: La Domenica del Corriere, July 9, 1961.

Morrow, Hugh. "The Success of an Utter Failure (Charles Schulz / Peanuts)." *Saturday Evening Post,* Jan. 12, 1957, 34–35, 70–72.

Muradov, Roman. "Fashion." *kuš!* #22. Riga, Latvia: n.p., Aug. 2015.

Murat, Thierry. *Le Vieil Homme et La Mer (The Old Man and the Sea).* Paris: Futuropolis, 2014.

Murphy, Stephen, author, and Michael Zulli, artist. "Stirrings." *Puma Blues* #3. Kitchener, ON: Aardvark-Vanaheim, Dec. 1986.

Oji, Hiroi, author, and Ryoichi Ikegami, artist. "The Kumamaru Chronicles." *Samurai Crusader* 1, no. 1. San Francisco: Viz Media, 1996.

———. "Way of the Dragon." *Samurai Crusader* 1, no. 8. San Francisco: Viz Communications, 1997.

———. "Sunrise over Shanghai." *Samurai Crusader* 2, no. 8–3, no. 5. San Francisco: Viz Communications, 1997.

"Our Ideas of Heaven." *Tabula* Yearbook. Oak Park, IL: Oak Park and River Forest High School, 1917.

Naylor, Jim. *Ernest Hemingway,* Aug. 9, 2011. www.Cartoonstock.com.

Palazzi, Marco. "Un giorno perfetto" (A Perfect Day). *Topolino* #2357. Modena: Mondadori, Disney Italia, Panini Comics, 2001.

Parrish, R. E. *Writer Fights.* 2014–16. https://reparrishcomics.com/.

Park, W. B. *"Like Hemingway, I Believe in Grace under Pressure—Unless, of Course, Things Get Too Hot." New Yorker,* Mar. 23, 1987.

Pesados, Pesos. *Heavy Weights,* illustration. Tucumán, Argentina: La Gaceta, Aug. 13, 2013.

Peterson, Eric, and Ethan Nicolle, artist. "A Hollow Cost." *Jesus Christ: In the Name of the Gun* #1. N.p.: Bad Karma Productions, Oct. 2009.

Perina, Alessandro. "Bad Boys." *Topolino* #2349. Modena: Mondadori, Disney Italia, Panini Comics. 2000.

Pett, Mark. *Lucky Cow,* Oct. 2, 2003. https://licensing.andrewsmcmeel.com /features/luc?date=2003-10-02.

Pozza, Luca. "Laguna Hemingway." Work in progress.

Pratt, Hugo. "Un Bolide a Reaction." *Pif Gadget* #1381. Paris: Editions Vaillant, Nov. 1971.

———. "Under the Flag of Gold." *Corto Maltese: Celtic Tales.* Paris: Casterman, 1972.

Price, Hilary. "Classics Update." *Rhymes with Orange,* Aug. 11, 2006.

———. "The Louvre." *Rhymes with Orange,* Aug. 22, 2008.

Quintanilla, Paul. "Portraits of Friends." *The Art and World of Louis Quintanilla.* http://www.lqart.org/portsfold/portfriends.html.

Rangel, Fabian, author, and Warwick Johnson-Caldwell, artist. *Helena Crash* #4. San Diego, CA: IDW Publishing, Oct. 2017.

Razook, Brad. "Lives of the Great." *National Lampoon Magazine,* Apr. 1979.

Razzi, Manuela. "Nelle acque" (In the Water). *Topolino* #2365. Modena: Mondadori, Disney Italia, Panini Comics, 2001.

Roca, Paco. *Twists of Fate.* Seattle, WA: Fantagraphics, 2018.

Rokuda, Noboru. 老人と海 (*The Old Man and the Sea*). N.p.: eBookJapan, 2014.

Saunders, Allen. *A Few Slightly Irreverent Epitaphs,* May 28, 2012. www.Cartoon stock.com

Scala, Guido. "Zio Paperone e . . . il vecchio e il mare" (Uncle Scrooge and the Old Man and the Sea). *Topolino* #1642. Modena: Mondadori, Disney Italia, Panini Comics, May 1987.

Schorr, Bill. *The Grizzwells,* Jan. 6, 1997. https://licensing.andrewsmcmeel.com /features/gw?date=1997-01-06.

———. *The Grizzwells,* July 8, 2014. https://licensing.andrewsmcmeel.com /features/gw?date=2014-07-08.

Schultz, Charles. *Peanuts,* Aug., 28 1984. https://licensing.andrewsmcmeel .com/features/pe?date=1984-08-28.

Schwadron, Harley. *"You're Lucky to Have Your Case Tried by Judge Hemingway. He's Known for His Short Snappy Sentences,"* Feb. 11, 2019. www.Cartoon stock.com.

———. *"Which Wine Goes Best with 'The Old Man and the Sea'?"* Jan. 2, 2014. www.Cartoonstock.com.

Scott, Jerry, author, and Jim Borgman, artist. *Zits,* May 20–22, 1999.

Seal, Bob. *"His Exercise Wheel Had Lost All Its Fascination Since He Started Reading Hemingway,"* Aug. 13, 2001. www.Cartoonstock.com.

Searle, Ronald. *Crossed Paths. New Yorker,* May 6, 1991.

Sebock, Imre. "The Short Happy Life of Francis Macomber." *Fules,* 1975.

Serra, Antonio, author; Nando Esposito, artist; and Denisio Esposito, artist. "Fantasmi a Venezia" (Ghost in Venice). *Speciale Nathan Never* #4. Milan: Sergio Bonelli Editore, Nov. 1994.

Shiriagari, Kotobuki. *Tanizaki Kaleidoscope: A Tanizaki Jun'ichiro Manga Anthology.* Tokyo: Chuo Koron Shinsha, 2016.

Sim, Dave, author, and Gerhard, artist. *Cerebus* #251–61. Kitchener, ON: Aardvark-Vanaheim, 2000.

———. *Cerebus* #262–65. Kitchener, ON: Aardvark-Vanaheim, 2001.

Sisti, Alessandro, author, and Graziano Barbaro, artist. "Per Chi Suona il Campanello?" (For Whom the Doorbell Tolls). *Topolino* #2278. Milan: Mondadori, Disney Italia, Panini Comics, July 1999.

Solis, Gustavo, author; Arq Fernando Gay, author; and Eduardo Martinez, artist. "Ernest Hemingway." *Vidas Ilustres* #102. Mexico City: Editorial Novaro, July 1964.

"Some Things We'll Miss." *Tabula* Yearbook. Oak Park, IL: Oak Park and River Forest High School, 1917.

Sono, Sanae. *The Old Man and the Sea.* Tokyo: Manga Bunko, 2011.

Specter, Irving. "Across the Old Man and Into the Sea." *Coogy. New York Herald-Tribune,* 1953.

sTone, benjamin. *Hemingway Comix,* Aug. 2011. Original website discontinued; now available on sTone's Flickr page, https://www.flickr.com/photos /benchilada/2657281974.

Stopeck, Marc. "Oak Park River Forest Literary Society," *Answer Book.* Oak Park, IL: Wednesday Journal, 2017.

———. *Shrubtown, Wednesday Journal,* Feb. 12, 2013. https://www.oakpark .com/News/Articles/2-12-2013/Shrubtown-_-Feb.-13,-2013/.

Thaves, Bob. "Creative Writing 101." *Frank and Ernest,* Oct. 17, 2003. https:// licensing.andrewsmcmeel.com/features/fk?date=2003-10-17.

———. *Frank and Ernest,* May 11, 1999. https://licensing.andrewsmcmeel .com/features/fk?date=1999-05-11.

Thaves, Tom. *Frank and Ernest,* June 2, 2016. https://licensing.andrewsmc meel.com/features/fk?date=2016-06-02.

———. *Frank and Ernest,* June 27, 2018. https://licensing.andrewsmcmeel .com/features/fk?date=2018-06-27.

Thompson, Mike. *Grand Avenue,* Aug. 22, 2000. https://licensing.andrewsmc meel.com/features/gr?date=2000-08-22.

Thompson, Richard. "Signals of a Misspent Youth." *Richard's Poor Almanac,* July 22, 2015. https://licensing.andrewsmcmeel.com/features/rpa?date=2015-07-22.

———. "There's an Opossum in My Garage!" *Richard's Poor Almanac,* Apr. 4, 2011. https://licensing.andrewsmcmeel.com/features/rpa?date=2011-04-04.

———. "Thoughtful Last-Minute Father's Day Gifts." *Richard's Poor Almanac,* June 20, 2015. https://licensing.andrewsmcmeel.com/features/ rpa?date=2015-06-20.

Tomasi, Peter, author, and Doug Mahnke, artist. "Battlefield of Love." *Superman / Wonder Woman* #13. New York: DC Comics, Jan. 2015

Toomey, Jim. *Sherman's Lagoon,* Aug. 1, 2010.

Tosolini, Nicola. "Sahara." *Topolino* #2369. Modena: Mondadori, Disney Italia, Panini Comics, 2001.

Trudeau, Garry. *Doonesbury,* Jan. 18, 1977. https://licensing.andrewsmcmeel .com/features/db?date=1977-01-18.

———. *Doonesbury,* Apr. 5, 1981. https://licensing.andrewsmcmeel.com/ features/db?date=1981-04-05.

———. *Doonesbury,* Jan. 23, 1994. https://licensing.andrewsmcmeel.com/features/db?date=1994-01-23.

Turconi, Stefano. "Cowboy Blues." *Topolino* #2345. Modena: Mondadori, Disney Italia, Panini Comics, 2000.

Valtman, Edmund S. *The Old Man and the Sea. Hartford Times,* Oct. 31, 1972. Available at the *Library of Congress Prints and Photographs Online Catalog,* http://www.loc.gov/pictures/item/2016687295/.

Vance, Steve, author, and Rick Geary, artist. "Fantasy Island." *The Big Book of Vice* #1. New York: Paradox Press, Jan. 1998.

Wallach, Eli, author, and Bernard Krigstein, artist. "Out of the Frying Pan and into the Soup." *Mad Magazine* #24. New York: EC, July 1955.

Wagner, Matt. *Grendel vs. the Shadow.* Milwaukie, OR: Dark Horse Comics, 2015.

Ware, Chris. *Heurtley House Poster* (Oak Park). 2012. Print. Historical Society of Oak Park and River Forest.

Wayne, Matt. "The Last Time I Saw Paris." *The Brave and the Bold* #24. New York: DC Comics, June 2007.

Whitehead, Bill. *"Change the Old Guy to a Young, Hunk Lifeguard Patrolling a Trendy Beach in a Speedboat and You May Have Something!"* Aug. 15, 2013. www.Cartoonstock.com.

Wildt, Chris. *"For Pete's Sake! Does He HAVE to Say 'For Whom the Bell Tolls' Every Time the Stock Market Closes???"* Nov. 5, 2006. www.Cartoonstock.com.

———. *"Has Anyone Ever Told You Your Tweets are Hemingwayesque?"* Aug. 30, 2013. www.Cartoonstock.com.

Williams, Robert, and S. Clay Wilson. "The Ugly Head." *Hysteria in Remission: The Comix and Drawings of Robert Williams.* Edited by Eric Reynolds. Seattle, WA: Fantagraphics, 2002.

Winick, Judd. "How the West Was Weened." *The Adventures of Barry Ween Boy Genius 2.0* #2. Portland, OR: Oni Press, Mar. 2000.

Yann, author, and André Juillard, artist. *Double 7.* Paris: Dargaud, 2018.

Yurkovich, David. *Death by Chocolate: Redux.* Marietta, GA: Top Shelf Productions, 2007.

Zapico, Alfonso. *James Joyce: Portrait of a Dubliner.* Dublin: O'Brien Press, 2013.

Ziegler, Jack. *Cafe Metro. New Yorker,* Aug. 19, 1974. Available online at *Jack Ziegler—New Yorker Cartoonist,* https://jackziegler.com/product/cafe-metro/.

———. *Meanwhile at the Cafe De La Mort . . . Ernest Hemingway Is Ridiculing Oscar Wilde's Wine Spritzer While Truman Capote Takes Notes. New Yorker,* Dec. 4, 1989.

Ziorni, Giuseppe. "Mickey e i due cuochi" (Mickey and the Two Cooks). *Topolino* #2361. Modena: Mondadori, Disney Italia, Panini Comic, 2000.

Index

Page references in **bold** refer to illustrations.